FRIENDS
IN THE WILD

FRIENDS IN

A Supplement to Childcraft—

THE WILD

The How and Why Library

World Book, Inc.
a Scott Fetzer company
Chicago London Sydney Toronto

Stanzas I and II from THE GOAT PATHS by James Stephens
By permission of The Society of Authors, Literary Representative of the
Estate of James Stephens.

World Book, Inc.
525 West Monroe
Chicago, IL 60661
http://www.worldbook.com

Library of Congress Cataloging-in-Publication Data
Friends in the wild.
        p.   cm.
    "A supplement to Childcraft—the how and why library."
    Includes bibliographical references and index.
    Summary: Describes various kinds of wild animals which live
in such places as mountains, grasslands, rain forests, deserts,
and oceans. Includes follow-up learning activities.
    ISBN 0-7166-0698-4
    1. Animals—Juvenile literature. [1. Animals.] I. World Book,
Inc. II. Childcraft.
QL49.F9155   1998
590—dc21   98-15397

Printed in the United States of America

1 2 3 4 5 6 7 8 9   02 01 00 99 98

Contents

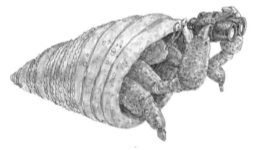

Staff

Preface

The lion prowls on padded paws,
Squirrels leap from limb to limb,
A fly can crawl straight up a wall,
Seals love to dive and swim.
Watch worms wiggle all around,
See the monkey swing by its tail.
The birds may hop upon the ground,
Or spread their wings and sail.

Animals get around in all kinds of ways, in part because they live in all different kinds of places. In this book, you will visit animal homes around the world—from high mountains, grasslands, forests, and deserts to polar regions, and even the ocean. In each place, you will see how the animals that live there get what they need—how they stay warm or cool, how they find shelter and food, raise young, and survive. The final chapter shows how people, animal habitats, and animals are all connected.

In each chapter, you'll find stories and poems to enjoy, as well as games, puzzles, and activities that will challenge your animal expertise! And check out the pages titled **A Closer Look.** Here you will find in-depth information on a variety of animals, such as eyeless cavefish and kitchen-loving cockroaches.

Throughout *Friends in the Wild,* interesting words are defined in the margins and in the **Glossary** at the back of the book. Also at the back is the **Index,** which lists what is in the book and on which pages to find it. For additional sources of information on animals and their habitats, see the section called **Find Out More.**

So now that you know about the good things inside this book, start turning the pages to learn all kinds of amazing things about your *Friends in the Wild.*

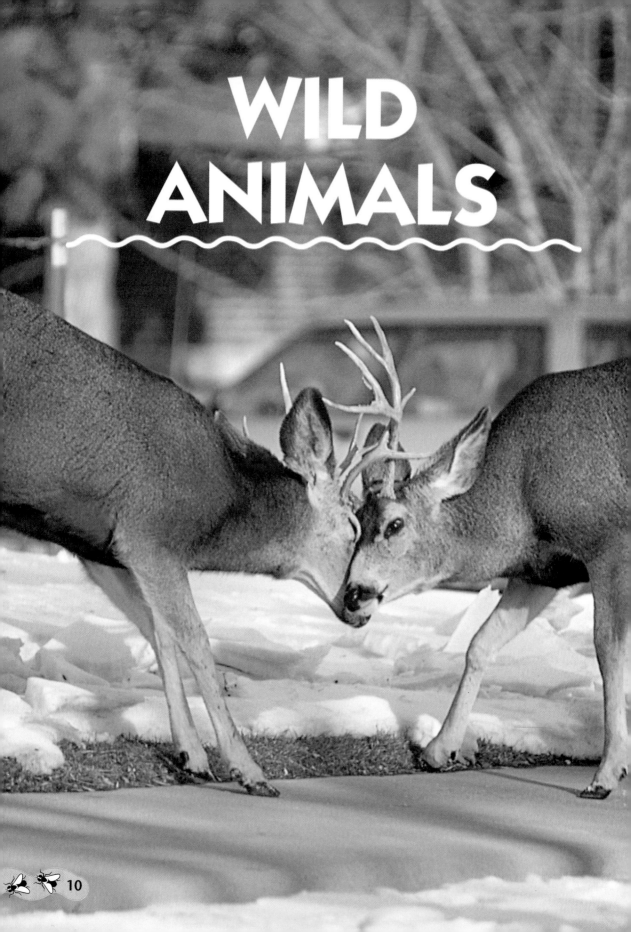

WILD ANIMALS

What are animals?

Everywhere in the world, you'll find animals. Some, like squirrels, parrots, and monkeys, have complex bodies and show many kinds of behaviors in different situations. Others are very simple, and many are too tiny to see. But all animals are connected to one another, to plants, and to their other surroundings in many ways.

What makes an animal an animal?

A jellyfish lives in the sea, has no bones, and looks a lot like an umbrella. A rhinoceros lives on land. It has a big, strong body, thick legs, and very little hair. But both are animals.

12

All animals are alike in some ways. Their bodies are made of cells—the building blocks of every living thing. But that isn't all they have in common. The jellyfish and rhinoceros move around. They sense when their surroundings change—for example, when something moves. They eat to survive. They take in oxygen. They try to defend themselves. All animals do these things.

Animals are also different in some ways. People who study them put them in groups—for example, animals that have backbones, and animals that do not. Animals with backbones, or vertebrae (VUHR tuh bree), are called vertebrates (VUHR tuh brihts). Animals without backbones are called invertebrates (ihn VUHR tuh brihts).

How are animals grouped?

Almost all animals are invertebrates. This group includes many ocean animals, such as sponges, jellyfish, starfish, and sea urchins. It also includes many land animals, such as insects, spiders, and snails. The animals within each of these smaller groups have things in common. Insects have six legs and usually have wings. Spiders have eight legs and no wings. Snails are mollusks—they have soft bodies and hard shells.

Warm-blooded means having blood that stays the same temperature regardless of the air temperature.

Cold-blooded means having blood that changes temperature according to the outside environment.

Vertebrates include amphibians, reptiles, birds, fish, and mammals. Frogs and other amphibians live partly on land and partly in water. Snakes and other reptiles are cold-blooded and have dry, scaly skin. Birds have feathers, and fish live in water. Mammals feed their young with the mother's milk.

You probably don't think of yourself as a kind of animal, but, just like a horse, a chimpanzee, or a skunk, you are—you're a mammal! As a mammal, you share many characteristics with all other animals. For example, like other animals, you can move and sense your surroundings. You also need to eat, breathe, and defend yourself from enemies.

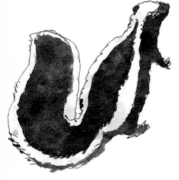

No one is sure how many kinds of animals exist. People know of about 1.5 million kinds. But there may be as many as 50 million kinds in the world.

Obviously, we have much to learn. Scientists are finding new kinds of animals all the time. In 1997, they found the smallest frog yet on the northern part of Earth. Called an eleuth (EHL yooth), the frog lives in Cuban forests. It is so small that four of these tiny frogs can sit on a nickel!

BIRDS

FISH

REPTILES

MAMMALS

INSECTS

AMPHIBIANS

MOLLUSKS

Where do animals live?

Animal homes

What do animals need to live? We know they don't need schools, stores, or post offices, but they do need some of the same things people need. To live, animals need a place that has food, water, and shelter, and that is safe enough to raise their young.

Pets, farm animals, and work animals are domestic (duh MEHS tihk) animals. They live around people and they depend on people for their food, water, and shelter. Wild animals also need food, water, and shelter, but they can provide these things for themselves. The places where wild animals can live and find what they need are called their habitats (HAB uh tats). An animal's habitat is its natural home.

Earth has many habitats. There are cold, windy, rocky mountains; open prairies; wet, muggy tropical rain forests; forests with changing seasons; dry deserts; wintry polar regions; and salty oceans. Animals live in every one of these places.

Each habitat has its special problems. Animals in polar regions must survive harsh winters. Desert creatures must live with little water. But the animals in each habitat can find what they need to survive. You won't find a shark living in a desert, and you won't find an elephant on a mountaintop. Why? Because they wouldn't survive there. A shark's habitat is the ocean, and an elephant's habitat is grasslands or forests.

Many kinds of animals live in South America. Some live in tropical rain forests, some in grasslands, some in mountains, and others in deserts.

Animals live in the habitat that's best for them

Over many thousands of years, animals have changed or adapted (uh DAP tihd) to fit their habitat. Sometimes their bodies adapted. Sometimes they changed their habits. A musk ox has thick fur. Its body has adapted to help it stay warm through the winter. A desert lark gets all its water from eating leaves. Its behavior has adapted to help it get the moisture it needs.

Because some animals adapt to one particular habitat, they cannot live anywhere else. The giant panda, for example, eats nothing but bamboo shoots, which are only found in certain forests. A polar bear does well in harsh polar regions, but it can't live anywhere else.

However, many animals can live in more than one habitat. For example, certain ostriches can live in grasslands or deserts. And whether you are in Bangkok or Boston, you have probably shooed away a fly! They are well adapted to find food, water, and shelter in any habitat.

Many kinds of animals share a habitat. They can do this because their lives are different in some important way. For example, they eat different foods or sleep in different places. Chimpanzees and gorillas live in some of the same forests in Africa, but they eat different foods. The chimps eat mostly fruit, while gorillas eat mostly leaves and stems. Because they are not competing for the same food, they can share a habitat. So you see, animals live in habitats where they can find food, water, and shelter, and which are safe enough to raise their young.

Is there wildlife in towns?

If you live in a town or city, you may think wild animals live far away in the forests. But the fact is, you are surrounded by wildlife!

Fierce hunters, such as spiders and centipedes, may be roaming your house and neighborhood right now.

Rats and pigeons live in cities all over the world. Today, many animals from other habitats—such as deer, squirrels, raccoons, and even coyotes—are moving into cities or suburbs. Why are these places so popular?

In every habitat, animals look for food, water, shelter, and a place to raise young. Some animals find everything they need in cities where gardens, backyards, and parks abound in plants for animals to eat. Green, leafy suburbs remind deer of their natural browsing place—the forest edge.

Insect-eating birds, such as nighthawks and chimney swifts, hang out at places where heat rises, such as subway vents. The rising heat carries insects and spiders along with it, straight to the waiting birds.

Towns also abound in a new kind of animal food—garbage! Raccoons, rats, and pigeons have learned to eat almost everything.

21

City parks have lots of water in lakes, birdbaths, fountains, and gutters. In some Western American cities, coyotes drink from lawn sprinklers.

And towns are good places to find shelter. Heat from homes, offices, and cars makes cities a lot toastier than open land. Starlings like to nest beneath the roofs of buildings and in air vents.

Some animals find that cities are a great place to raise a family. In the wild, peregrine (PEHR uh grihn) falcons lay their eggs on cliffs or mountain ledges, but the rooftops and ledges of tall buildings do just as well!

Only certain animals are suited to city life, though. Generally, urban animals eat a wide variety of food. And they don't mind being around people. They're usually very smart and able to change their ways. For example, raccoons have learned how to open garbage cans and unlatch doors. In the forest, squirrels are very shy. But city squirrels beg and forage for food. When people rode horses, sparrows used to eat the horses' grain. Today, most people ride around in cars, so sparrows have learned to eat out of garbage cans and bird feeders.

Many wild animals adapt to city ways. On the opposite page, a raccoon forages for garbage at night, and a deer is at home in the grassy suburbs. Below, kangaroos forage through garbage in an Australian city.

23

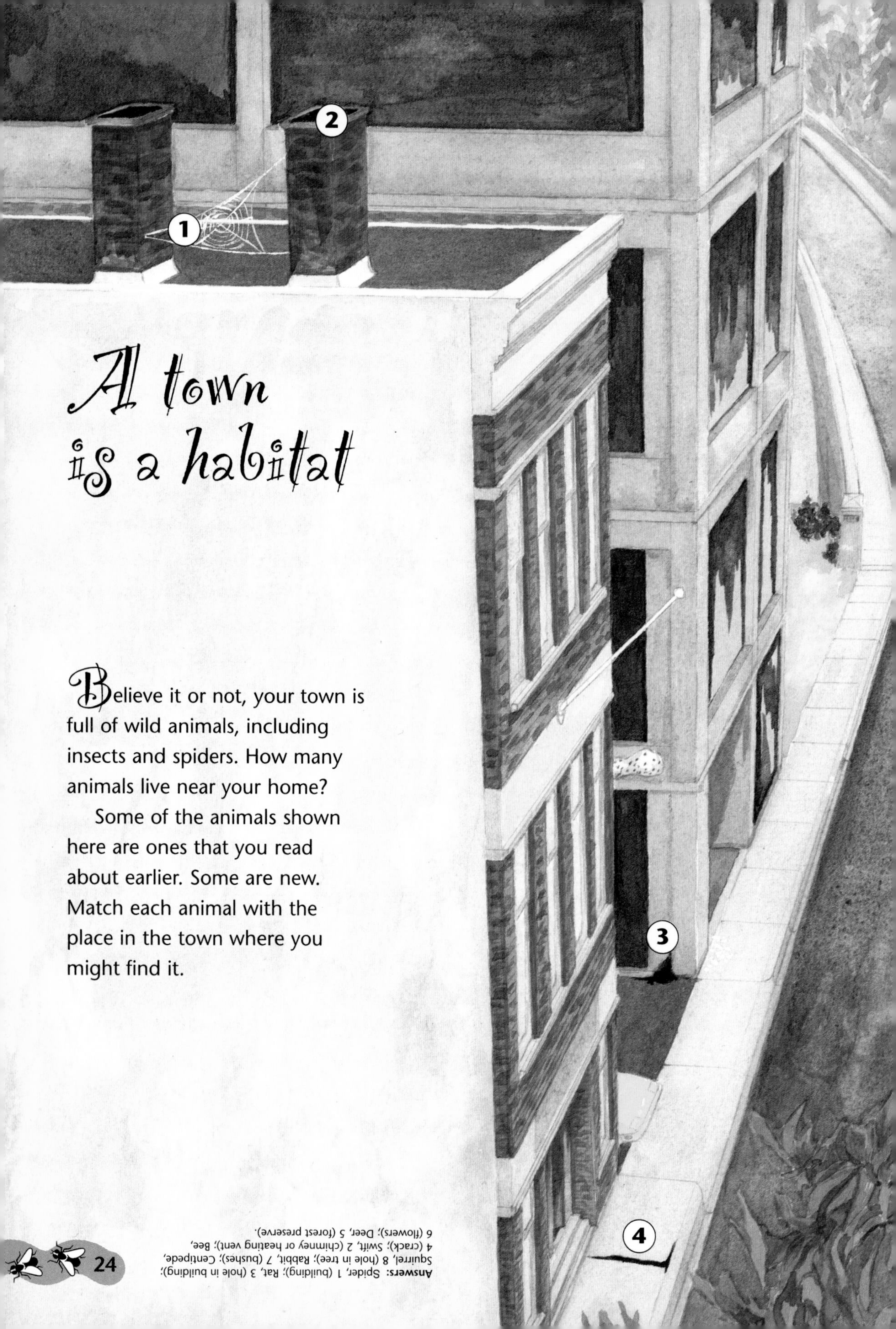

A town is a habitat

Believe it or not, your town is full of wild animals, including insects and spiders. How many animals live near your home?

Some of the animals shown here are ones that you read about earlier. Some are new. Match each animal with the place in the town where you might find it.

Answers: Spider, 1 (building); Rat, 3 (hole in building); Squirrel, 8 (hole in tree); Rabbit, 7 (bushes); Centipede, 4 (crack); Swift, 2 (chimney or heating vent); Bee, 6 (flowers); Deer, 5 (forest preserve).

5

6

7

8

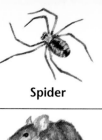
Spider

Rat

Squirrel

Rabbit

Centipede

Swift

Bee

Deer

What is a food chain?

On an African grassland, a zebra is nibbling plants. Swoosh—a lion pounces! The lion eats the zebra. Much later, when the lion dies, vultures feast on its body. Worms and termites feed on the leftovers. Tiny living things called bacteria and fungi break down the remains to feed the soil. Plants grow in the soil. A zebra nibbles the plants....

The plants, zebra, lion, vultures, worms, termites, bacteria, fungi, and soil are connected. Each of them is food for another. Together they make up a food chain.

Food chains are everywhere

Everywhere on Earth, plants and animals make up food chains. And in each food chain, they act in certain ways.

All plants are producers—from tiny Arctic mosses to giant rain forest trees. Plants make food, using energy from the sun.

All animals are consumers—from the smallest insect to the biggest blue whale. They eat food. Some consumers, such as rabbits or zebras, eat plants. Other consumers, such as foxes or lions, eat animals.

SOME HERBIVORES

Manatee   Japanese beetle   Green iguana

Animals that eat mostly or entirely plants are called herbivores (HUHR buh vawrz), which means "plant-eaters." Animals that eat mostly or entirely other animals are called carnivores (KAHR nuh vawrz), which means "meat-eaters." Animals that eat both plants and animals are called omnivores (AHM nuh vawrz), which means "all-eaters."

SOME CARNIVORES

Tiger

Spotted owl

King cobra

SOME OMNIVORES

Raven   Jerboa   Raccoon

Of course, food chains may be very long. A plant-eating insect may be caught by a small fish, which is eaten by a bigger fish, which is caught by a bird, which is caught by a fox. The fox is the last consumer—the top carnivore in the food chain.

Most animals are part of many food chains. These food chains overlap, linking all living things. They make up the web of life.

Predators and prey

You probably don't like to think of a fox killing a bird. The fox is a predator (PREHD uh tuhr). The bird is its prey (PRAY). But, believe it or not, species that are prey need predators.

Predators usually kill weak animals—the old or sick ones. The younger, faster, healthier animals escape. They are most likely to have healthy babies and keep their species growing.

Suppose all the foxes disappeared. The number of birds would increase, and there wouldn't be enough fish for them. Many birds would starve. But with predators in a habitat, there will be fewer prey. The balance of predators and prey keeps the web of life healthy.

29

Ultimate generalists and specialists

Animals that live in one habitat are called specialists (SPEHSH uh lihsts). They eat only certain foods and survive in certain climates. For example, Cape sugarbirds feed mostly from flowers on protea (PROH tee uh) shrubs. These shrubs grow only on mountains in southern Africa, so that's where the sugarbirds can live—nowhere else.

Animals that live in many habitats are called generalists (JEHN uhr uh lists). Flies, mice, and humans are generalists. We can eat all kinds of things and live in all kinds of weather.

Is it better to be a generalist or a specialist? That depends. If its habitat is thriving, a specialist is luckier. Why? There is less competition for food. But if a habitat is changing, a generalist has the best chance to survive.

The ultimate generalist is the cockroach. This insect lives everywhere— rain forests, deserts, caves, and houses. There are 3,500 kinds of cockroaches, some of which were here before the dinosaurs. Some scientists think cockroaches could survive a nuclear war.

It's no surprise that cockroaches live everywhere—they eat almost anything!

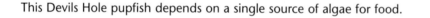

This Devils Hole pupfish depends on a single source of algae for food.

Why are cockroaches so successful? For a start, they eat everything, including shoe polish, glue, and human toenails! Inside their bodies, simple, one-celled creatures break down anything the cockroach eats. And if things get really bad, cockroaches can live for a month without food or water.

The ultimate specialist may be the Devils Hole pupfish. This tiny fish has been found in only one place, a spring in a Nevada cave called Devils Hole. It eats only algae (AL jee)—simple living things—that grow on an underwater ledge. For algae to grow, sunlight must shine on the water. If the water level goes down, sunlight misses the water, and the fish have nothing to eat.

About 300 to 900 pupfish live in Devils Hole. Others are being raised in captivity. They will continue the species if the pupfish at Devils Hole die out.

HIGH-MOUNTAIN ANIMALS

What is a mountain habitat?

On the treeless, snow-crusted slopes of a mountain in Tibet, a herd of huge, shaggy yaks fans out, pawing the snow to get at the plants below. With their long coats and short legs, the animals are built for warmth. Even their stomachs act as a kind of furnace. The food they eat heats up as it ferments, keeping them so warm that they seldom shiver. And these large, bulky, short-legged animals can move with surprising ease, sliding down a steep slope and

High mountains

then picking their way across a field of loose rock to reach the next frozen meadow.

On a forested mountain in North America, deer make their way down a trail. Heavy snow covers the high slopes, and they are looking for better grazing in warmer, lower places. High in a tree, a twig snaps, and the deer scatter. But it's too late. With a heavy thud, a mountain lion lands on a deer, pinning it to the ground. Today the mountain lion will have a good feed. Its last meal was only a badger.

Himalaya means "House of Snow" or "Snowy Range" in Sanskrit, an ancient language.

Deciduous comes from Latin words meaning "to fall away."

Every continent has mountains. Some of the largest and highest mountain ranges, such as the Rockies in North America, the Andes in South America, the Alps in Europe, and the Himalaya in Asia, have bare, snow-capped peaks. Smaller mountains are often covered with grasses, forests, or mosses and other small plants. In deserts, mountains may be mostly dry and stony.

Often a single mountain has many habitats. One side of a mountain may have different plants and animals from the other, because more rain falls there. Habitats may be different at different heights, too.

At the base of many mountains, the weather is mild. Deciduous (dih SIHJ oo uhs) trees—like oaks and maples—grow there. These trees lose their leaves every autumn (also called fall) and grow new leaves in the spring. In tropical climates, rain forests may cover the lower slopes. In desert areas, tough grasses and bushes may grow.

Higher up in many mountain ranges, deciduous trees mix with coniferous (kuh NIHF uhr uhs) trees, such as spruce, fir, and pine. These cone-bearing trees keep their needlelike leaves year-round.

Deciduous forest

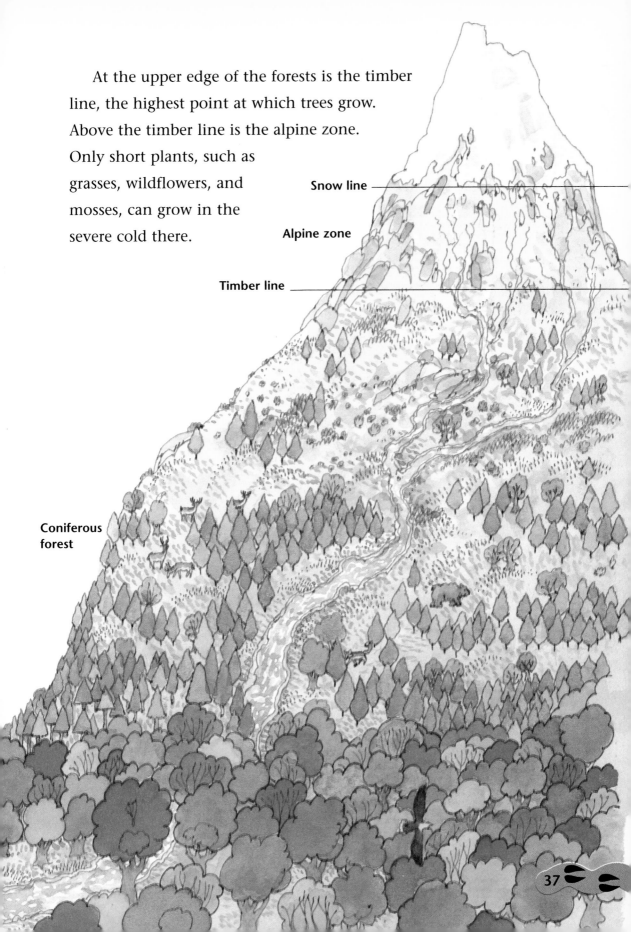

At the upper edge of the forests is the timber line, the highest point at which trees grow. Above the timber line is the alpine zone. Only short plants, such as grasses, wildflowers, and mosses, can grow in the severe cold there.

Snow line

Alpine zone

Timber line

Coniferous forest

Above the alpine zone is the snow line. There the air is very cold. Snow and ice cover the peaks. There are no plants, and the only animals are birds and insects. Golden eagles and condors soar over mountains. Bar-headed geese cross the Himalaya in their yearly migrations, and Nepalese swifts live there. Insects are whisked up the mountains by the strong winds. The common Apollo butterfly uses its strong wings to soar on wind currents in Scandinavia, the Alps, and the Pyrenees.

Many animals live on mountain slopes. In North America and Europe, you can find bears, deer, elk, foxes, trout in streams, and insects. In eastern Africa, mountain gorillas live in cool mountain forests.

Some plant-eaters, such as vicuñas in South America and yaks in Tibet, live above the timber line, in the alpine zone. So do smaller mammals, such as alpine marmots (a type of rodent) and pikas (related to rabbits). Plant-eating animals, such as deer, often move up the slopes in summer and down in winter, wherever food is plentiful.

Snow line is the line on mountains above which there is always snow.

Vicuña (vih KOON yuh) is a relative of the camel.

The Goat Paths

by James Stephens

The crooked paths
Go every way
Upon the hill
—They wind about
Through the heather,
In and out
Of a quiet
Sunniness.

And the goats
Day after day
Stray
In sunny quietness;
Cropping here,
And cropping there
—As they pause,
And turn,
And pass—
Now a bit
Of heather spray
Now a mouthful
Of the grass.

In the deeper
Sunniness,
In the place
Where nothing stirs;
Quietly
In quietness;
In the quiet
Of the furze
They stand awhile;
They dream;
They lie;
They stare
Upon the roving sky.

If you approach
They run away!
They will stare,
And stamp,
And bound,
With a sudden angry
sound,
To the sunny
Quietude:
To crouch again,
Where nothing stirs;
In the quiet
Of the furze.
To crouch them down
Again,
And brood
In the sunny
Solitude.

Vicuñas are adapted to life at very high altitudes. Their hearts are large, efficient pumps that help their blood circulate quickly.

Surviving high altitudes

Living high on a mountain is hard for most people because it is cold and the air up there is "thin." That means there is less oxygen (AHK suh juhn) high on a mountain than there is lower down. We need to breathe oxygen.

Mountain climbers and researchers doing mountain field work need special equipment to stay warm, and they sometimes need tanks of oxygen to breathe. Yet some animals live well in this rugged environment. So what do they have that we don't? Their bodies are special in some way. They have adapted to their mountain home.

In thin air

The vicuña lives in the Andes of South America. It has an extra-large heart. Blood picks up oxygen from the lungs and carries it to all parts of the body. Even though there is less oxygen in the high mountain air, the vicuña's big heart pumps blood

Ox is any member of a large group of animals that includes cattle and buffalo.

through its body quickly. This helps the vicuña get the oxygen it needs.

The yak is a kind of wild ox that lives very high up in the mountains of Tibet. It is taller than most people and weighs up to 1,200 pounds (544 kilograms). The yak can live in the thin mountain air because its blood holds lots of oxygen.

Yaks survive in cold mountains with oxygen-poor air. They have blood that stores the oxygen they take in.

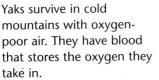

Real-life cliffhangers

Climbing rocks is hard for people, but not for the sure-footed animals that live there. Yaks, for example, have short, sturdy legs and padded hoofs that help them grip the rock going down steep slopes and across rocky places.

The rock hyrax lives in the mountains of Africa. This animal, only about the size of a rabbit, has feet that can stick to rocks! The soles have damp rubbery pads. When the rock hyrax climbs, it sucks in the middle of its soles. This makes its feet stick to the rocks like suction cups.

When the mountain goat of North America runs up cliffs, its hoofs spread apart to grip the rock. In 20 minutes it can climb about 1,500 feet (450 meters). That's over 100 stories—and higher than the world's tallest skyscrapers!

Other mountain animals are helped by long legs. Mountain lions—also called pumas or cougars— live in North and South America. They can jump 50 feet (15 meters) down a cliffside. That's like jumping off a five-story building!

In China, the Reeves pheasant lives in mountain forests. This bird can fly, but it is known for using its long legs to walk. It even runs uphill!

Food, water, and warmth

Animals that live on high mountains work hard to find food. Snow leopards in Tibet hunt anything that moves—from rats to yaks. They eat every bit of the prey except bones and skin! Large, hairy wolf spiders are excellent hunters. They chase down the insects they eat.

Giant pandas in the mountains of China eat bamboo—by the ton. Their large, flat back teeth and strong jaws help them chew the tough leaves and stems. Yunnan (YOO nan) snub-nosed monkeys also live in China. Besides leaves, they eat lichen, which is plentiful in mountain areas.

This wolf spider is large, hairy, and fast on its feet.

Strong teeth and grasping paws help pandas handle a diet of bamboo.

To keep warm, small rodents called chinchillas grow the thickest fur of any animal.

When food is scarce, the chamois (SHAM ee), a European relative of the goat, may have to go without food for two weeks or more. And high in the Andes, where there is little water, chinchillas get all the moisture they need from herbs that hold dew.

Keeping warm is another problem. Many mountain animals grow thick fur. Chinchillas have the thickest fur of any animal.

All of these animals can survive because they are warm-blooded. But you won't find snakes in cold mountain areas because reptiles are cold-blooded. Cold-blooded animals depend on the outside temperature to keep their bodies warm and active.

Hibernating and migrating

Hibernate is a word that comes from a Latin word meaning "winter."

When food is scarce and the weather is cold, some animals hibernate (HY buhr nayt)—they simply sleep through the winter. During the summer, they eat a lot and get fat. Then, when it's cold, they sleep. While they are sleeping, they live off their extra fat.

Marmots live in Europe, Asia, and North America. They are members of the squirrel family. When winter gets close, they dig underground rooms, or burrows, and fill them with hay. Then as many as twelve marmots cuddle up together and sleep all winter.

Himalayan black bears live in Asia's mountain forests. They sleep for part of the winter in a cave or a tree hole. When they're awake, they like to sun themselves in a nest of twigs in the snow.

Other animals migrate (MY grayt)—they move
to a place where there is more food in winter.
Wild goats called ibexes live in the
mountains of Europe, the Middle East, Asia,
and Africa. During the winter, ibexes
move down the mountains to find
food where there is less snow.
Snow leopards, which
follow the ibexes,
sometimes come close
enough to villages
to prey on tame
goats.

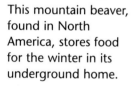

This mountain beaver, found in North America, stores food for the winter in its underground home.

Summer and winter

Besides hibernating and migrating, mountain animals find other ways to live through the cold winters. Some animals save food during the summer. The red fox buries food in summer and digs it up in winter. The mountain beaver of North America stores plants in its underground home and eats heartily when winter comes.

Many animals change their appearance in winter to avoid predators. Some, like the ermine (a weasel) in Europe and Asia and certain birds in Alaska and Greenland, grow white coats. The color blends in with the snow, helping them hide.

Many animals keep warm the way you do—by putting on a warm winter coat. But they grow their own! Red deer, which live in Europe, Asia, and North Africa, grow a longer coat in winter. Mountain goats grow a winter coat that is 8 inches (20 centimeters) long.

California condors are big birds in big trouble. Pollution, pesticides, and humans moving into their territory have nearly made them extinct. Now they are being bred in captivity, but they need to be returned to the wild. To help, scientists have turned to South America's Andean condor.

Since the two species are similar, the more plentiful Andean condors are being raised and released into California's mountains. Studying their responses helps scientists learn how to ease California condors back to living in the wild.

Many animals, such as this red deer, grow a longer, warmer coat in the winter. They shed it for a lighter coat in summer.

Mountain mammals

Here are some of the world's major mountain ranges. Pick a mountain mammal and score 1 point for naming each range where it can be found.

Earn an extra point for matching the animal to its adaptation below:

a. has a big heart

b. hides food underground in summer

c. coat gets longer in winter

d. migrates down mountain in winter

e. hair turns white in winter

f. has the thickest fur of any animal

g. has sturdy legs, padded hoofs, and blood that holds lots of oxygen

h. has strong teeth and jaws to chew bamboo

i. hibernates in the winter

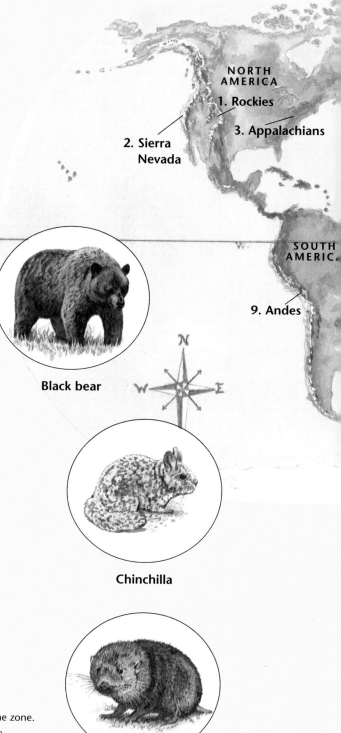

NORTH AMERICA
1. Rockies
3. Appalachians
2. Sierra Nevada

SOUTH AMERICA

9. Andes

Black bear

Chinchilla

Mountain beaver

Scoring
25–33 points: You're flying high with the eagles.
16–24 points: You're with snow leopards in the alpine zone.
8–15 points: You're living just below the timber line.
0–7 points: You're down in the grasslands, looking up.

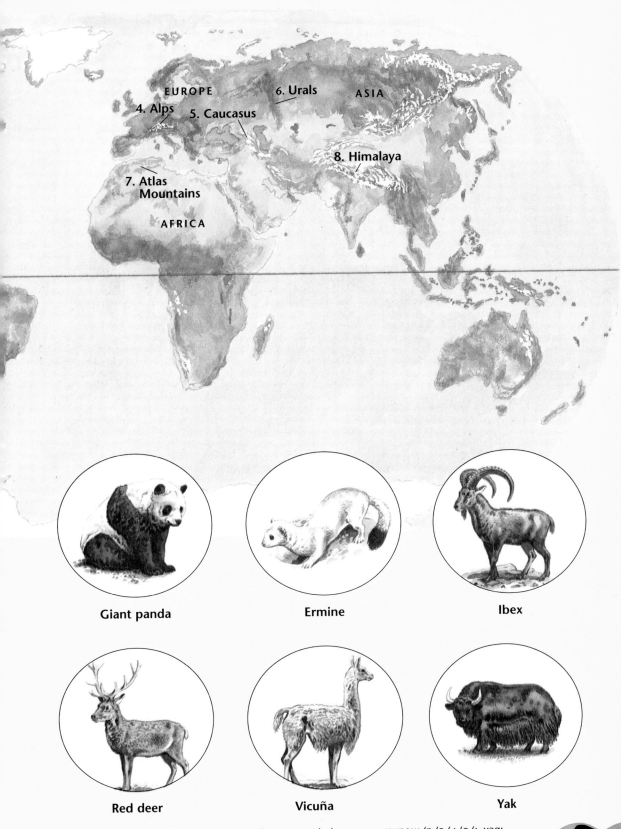

EUROPE

ASIA

6. Urals

4. Alps

5. Caucasus

8. Himalaya

7. Atlas
Mountains

AFRICA

Giant panda

Ermine

Ibex

Red deer

Vicuña

Yak

Answers: Black bear 1, 2, 3, 4, 5, 6, 8, i; Chinchilla 9, f; Giant panda 8, h; Ermine 4, 5, 6, e;
Ibex 4, 5, 7, 8, d; Mountain beaver 2, b; Red deer 4, 5, 6, 7, 8, c; Vicuña 9, a; Yak 8, g

53

Eagles

An eagle in flight, with its wings outstretched, is a wondrous sight. And today, more people are seeing these awesome birds. With conservation efforts underway, the population of this bird is increasing.

The golden eagle gets its name from the golden feathers on its neck and head. It is found in the mountains of North America, Asia, and northern Africa. With its powerful wings, it can soar above mountains to hunt its prey.

The Verreaux's eagle lives in the mountains of Africa. It's a specialist—it eats only small animals called rock hyraxes.

The bald eagle of North America is the national bird of the United States. But it is not really bald—its head is covered with white feathers. The bald eagle also can fly high above mountains. However, it spends much of its time near water, hunting for its favorite food—fish.

Bald eagle

All eagles have strong wings and wingspans that measure 4 to 8 feet (1.2 to 2.4 meters). They also have excellent hearing and very sharp eyes—ten times sharper than human eyes. This makes them excellent hunters.

To spot their prey easily, eagles hunt only during the day. They use their long, curved talons (claws) and their powerful hooked beaks to catch and eat smaller animals.

After hunting, eagles return to their nests, called aeries (AIR eez). Most eagles nest far from predators, including people, in high, hard-to-reach places. Bald eagles build in the tops of tall trees or on cliffs. Golden eagles usually nest on cliffs in the mountains. Eagles often return to the same aerie year after year, building it up each time.

Eagle aerie

In the wild, eagles can live up to 30 years. However, the females lay only one or two eggs each year and usually raise only one chick. So their numbers do not increase rapidly. In many places, eagles and their habitats need protection to survive.

Golden eagle

GRASSLAND ANIMALS

What are grasslands?

Beneath the wide blue sky, grasses ripple for miles. A carpet of colorful wildflowers stretches as far as the eye can see. Out of the bright yellow center of a flower comes a bumblebee, rear end first, covered with pollen. Prairie dogs sit on their haunches, chewing blades of grass, while one stands guard on a mound of dirt nearby. A hawk circles overhead. A quick bark from the lookout says "Danger!" and the other prairie dogs scurry into their holes.

Grasslands

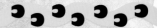

Pronghorn is a horned and hoofed animal that looks like an antelope. The fastest mammal in the Western Hemisphere, it runs at speeds up to 60 miles (96 km) per hour.

North American grasslands

Bright flames flicker in the distance. Fire! A group of pronghorn look up from their grazing. A distant rumble signals a herd of animals running. Soon the fire will sweep across the entire grassland, but the fire will not destroy it. Most grassland animals are well prepared to escape safely. Many, such as rodents and snakes, hide in their burrows. Other animals are equipped to run or fly away. The fire removes unwanted weeds. Its ashes will fertilize the soil, and the grasses will easily grow again to feed the animals.

African grasslands

Grasslands are not wet enough to be forests and not dry enough to be deserts. But the rainfall is just right for grasses, and grasslands are rich with plant and animal life.

Tropical grasslands are warm all year round. They usually have a rainy season and a dry season. In some, such as the African savanna, there is enough rain for a few trees to grow. Temperate grasslands have hot summers and cold winters. Grasslands support many kinds of plant-eating animals and predators. The Pampas, vast grasslands, stretch across parts of South America. Rodents such

as the mara forage there. They are food for meat-eaters such as pumas, Pampas cats, and large weasels called grisons.

The grasses, bushes, and trees of the African savanna feed many large plant-eaters, including the zebra, giraffe, wildebeest (WIHL duh BEEST), elephant, and rhinoceros. Large meat-eaters, such as lions and cheetahs, hunt them.

In the outback of Australia, the largest grass-eaters are kangaroos and wallabies. The only hunter is the dingo, a wild dog. Large, flightless birds called emus share the same territory.

Many grasslands are ideal for farming. Some, like the great prairies of North America where bison once grazed, have all but disappeared. Today, however, many countries preserve grasslands.

How and what do grassland animals eat?

The world's greatest populations of large animals live on the savannas of Africa. How can there be enough food for so many huge animals?

Mostly vegetarians here

With its wide, square mouth, the hippo mows the grass close as it feeds.

In the savannas, most animals are herbivores—plant-eaters. They eat trees, grass, leaves, seeds, and fruits, but not other animals. If they all ate the same thing at the same time, there would not be enough to go around. Luckily, savanna animals eat different kinds of plants or eat at different times. And plants keep growing!

Many plant-eaters are grazers—they eat grass. Some grazers prefer the tips of grass. Others, such as the hippopotamus and white rhinoceros, have wide, square lips for cropping grass close to the ground.

Many grazers migrate from place to place in search of food. When one type of grazer leaves an area, another animal usually arrives to eat the leftovers. For example, buffalo like marsh grasses that grow tall after the rains. When the buffalo move to another place, the grass begins to sprout again. Then other grazers, such as elands and zebras, arrive to dine on the tender new plants.

Hippopotamus—The name of this short-legged, thick-bodied animal comes from two Greek words that mean "horse" and "river."

Rhinoceros—The rhinoceros gets its name from Greek words that mean "nose horn." All species of rhinoceros have either one or two horns on their noses.

A Cape buffalo grazes on tall plants.

Black rhinos

A giraffe browses on high branches of a thorny tree.

Twigs and shrubs—Yum!

Other savanna plant-eaters are browsers. Browsers munch on the leaves, bark, twigs, and pods of trees and shrubs. Some plants, such as acacias and thornbushes, have sharp thorns, but many browsers have pointy snouts. They can easily avoid the thorns and pick out the leaves.

Giraffes have adapted in another way. They have saliva as thick as rubber cement, which protects the inside of their mouths from thorns. Their thick lips

protect the outside of their mouth from the thorns.

A long-necked antelope called the gerenuk (GUR uh nuk) has hip joints that are different from those of grazers. These joints enable it to stand for long periods on its hind legs to reach leaves. The black rhinoceros uses its flexible upper lip to grasp and pluck leaves. And it can eat plants that are highly irritating to other grazers.

A gerenuk stands upright to reach a meal.

HELPING HANDS

Harvest mice in the grasslands of England don't play tennis, but they sure like tennis balls! Scientists use tennis balls to help them find out if farming reduces the number of these mice in the fields. Since it is hard to spot tiny mice in big fields, doing a mouse count without the help of tennis balls would be quite a job. Tennis balls with small holes in them are tossed into the fields, and the mice happily make their nests inside the balls. They make perfect homes for mice and they make critter counting possible for scientists.

The eating chambers

Grass and leaves are nourishing, but they are hard to chew and even harder to digest. Plant-eaters are well-adapted, however. They have large, flat teeth for grinding up the plants. They also have special bacteria in their stomachs. The bacteria break down the grass and leaves so that the animal can use the food for energy.

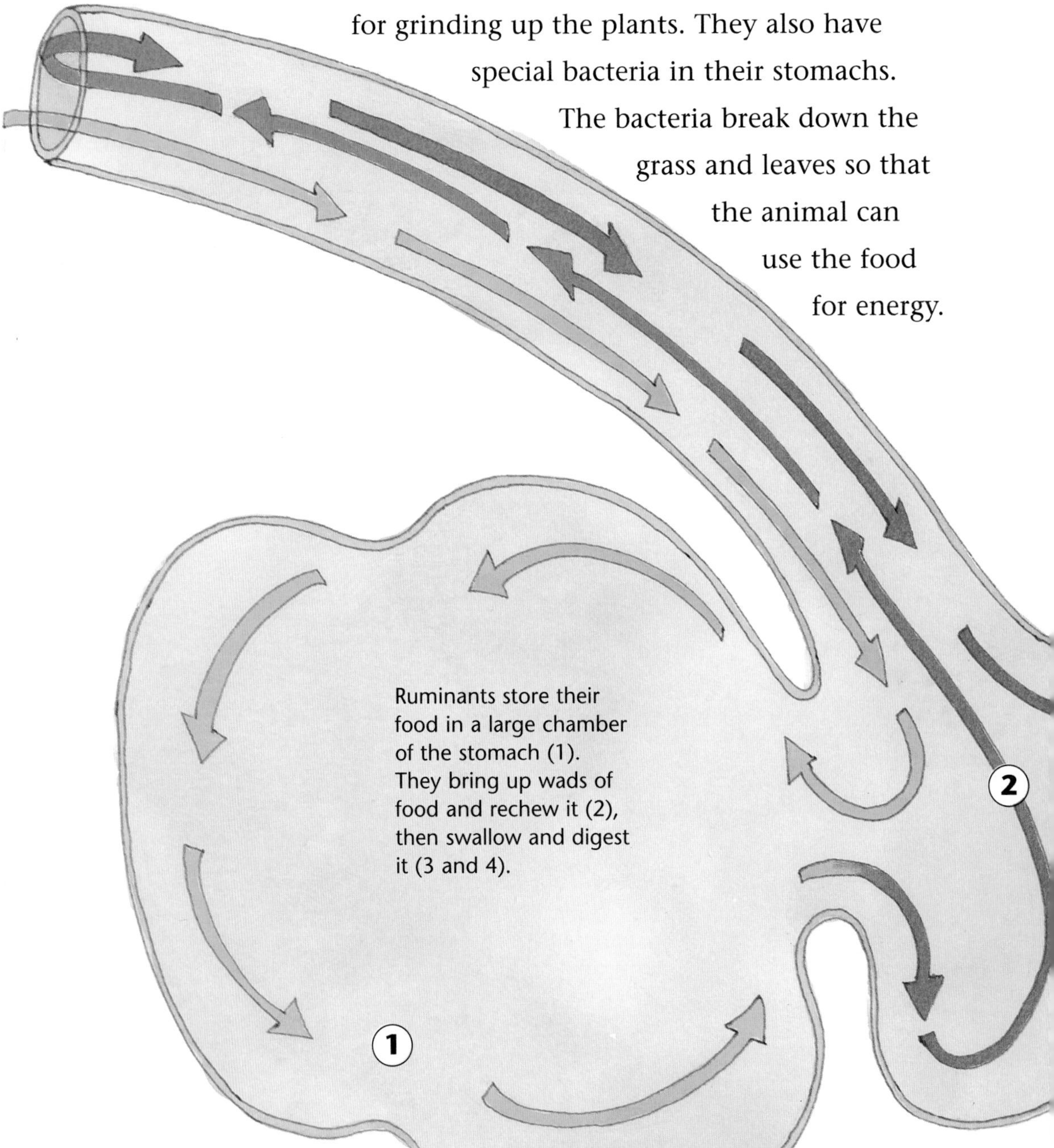

Ruminants store their food in a large chamber of the stomach (1). They bring up wads of food and rechew it (2), then swallow and digest it (3 and 4).

2

1

Does it seem that grazing animals are always eating? Well, they almost always are. Many plant-eaters, including buffalo, giraffes, and antelopes, are ruminants (ROO muh nuhnts), like cows. Their stomachs are divided into four separate chambers to digest tough plant material. While grazing, a ruminant swallows its food quickly, chewing it only slightly and keeping a lookout for danger. The food is stored in one of the chambers of its stomach.

Later, when the animal is resting, its stomach sends the food, now called cud, up to its mouth to be chewed and mixed with saliva. Then the animal swallows the food again. It goes to the other chambers of the stomach, gets digested, and then passes through the body.

Buffalo is one of several kinds of oxen, such as the Cape buffalo of Africa or the water buffalo of Asia. The large, shaggy bison of North America is also called a buffalo, but it is not a true buffalo.

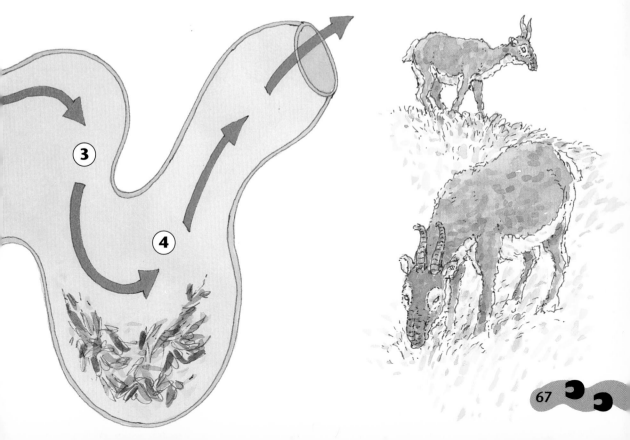

A cheetah puts on a burst of speed to run down its prey in a herd of wildebeest.

Meals for meat-eaters

Meat-eaters need to be fast or very clever to catch a meal! If they are not, they may not get dinner. Some of the fastest-moving mammals live in the grasslands, where there are large open spaces for running but few places to hide. Meat-eaters always look for easy targets, such as slow, sick, or injured animals. They do this to save their energy. They cannot be sure when they will eat their next meal.

The lion is the top carnivore of the African savanna. Lions live in family groups called prides. The males guard the cubs while the less conspicuous female lions hunt, usually at night. A lion creeps up on its prey until it is

Wildebeest is a large antelope that is one of the fastest animals in southern Africa. In Afrikaans, a Dutch-African language, its name means "wild beast." It is also known by its African name, *gnu.*

close enough to charge and grab the animal or knock it down.

The other big cats, cheetahs and leopards, are built for speed. They have long legs and flexible backs. A cheetah's claws grip the ground like cleats on athletic shoes. Cheetahs hunt by day, running up to 70 miles (110 kilometers) an hour to chase down antelopes and gazelles.

African hunting dogs travel in groups of 10 to 40, leaving one female in the den to guard the pups. A pack will often surround a herd of grazers and try to separate one animal as its prey.

Pride is a family group of lions. Most prides have at least twice as many adult females as males. The females in a pride are usually related, but the males come from other groups.

Some animals enjoy leftovers

Hyenas are part hunter and part scavenger. Some species of hyenas are able to kill large animals. But they are always on the lookout for another hunter's leftovers—a free meal.

After the hunters and hyenas have eaten their fill, the vultures move in. Like plant-eating animals, different kinds of vultures have different eating behaviors. Some species of vultures have powerful beaks that can tear a carcass open and snap through tendons. Other species, such as white-backed vultures, plunge their long beaks and bald heads deep into a carcass to feed on the soft insides. Egyptian vultures use their narrow beaks to snatch up bits of meat left by the other birds.

Clearly, each savanna animal is well adapted to its own special place in the food chain. But in the end, all the animals depend on plants, especially the grasses.

Carcass (KAHR kuhs) is the body of a dead animal.

Between meals

In the heat of a summer day, many smaller grassland animals rest in cool burrows underground. Even a bird, the nesting owl, finds an empty burrow to use as its nest. Larger animals don't have burrows or trees for shade. They have other ways to beat the heat.

Kangaroos lick the inside of their forearms. This cools the blood vessels close to the skin. Elephants' ears are rich with

A kangaroo licks its forearms to cool off.

Snow and ice can't penetrate the thick winter coat of a North American buffalo.

Flapping its ears helps this elephant cool its blood.

blood vessels. They flap their huge ears to cool down. And rhinos and hippos do what you probably would do—they head to the nearest water hole to cool off.

Winter in temperate grasslands is bitterly cold, but animals survive. Some of them hibernate or go into deep winter sleep in holes or burrows. Some animals that don't sleep through winter, such as North American buffalo, grow a thick coat to keep warm. Other animals, particularly birds, migrate to warmer parts of the world.

Night stalkers

Grassland cats that creep up on their prey at night, such as the Pampas cat of Argentina and the lion of the African savanna, need to see well in the dark. Cats can see six times better than humans in dim light because they have a special mirrorlike layer, called a tapetum, at the back of each eye. The tapetum (tuh PEE tuhm) increases the amount of light that strikes the seeing cells inside the eye.

Make your own model of a cat's eye and see how the tapetum reflects light.

You will need
scissors
black construction paper
a large, clean can
masking tape
a flashlight
a friend

1. On the construction paper, trace a circle with a diameter about 1 inch (2.5 cm) larger than the diameter of the can. Cut out the circle.
2. Cut an oval-shaped opening in the middle of the circle.

3. Make sure that the can is clean and that the inside bottom is shiny. Cover the open end with the circle and tape the circle to the can.

4. In a dark room, have a friend hold the can with the slit facing you. Shine the flashlight at the slit. What do you see?

The pupils (the dark openings) of cats' eyes open very wide in the dark. To find out why, make two more circles. But make the opening of each one slightly wider than the one before it. Repeat the last two steps for each one. Which opening creates the greatest reflection?

Greater kudu

Hoofs and horns

Thompson's gazelle

Think about this: Have you ever seen an animal that has both claws and horns? Or one that has both hoofs and sharp teeth? Of course not—there are no such creatures. Only animals with hoofs grow horns. And hoofed animals don't have sharp teeth. Let's take a closer look at hoofed animals and find out why.

Almost all of the large plant-eating animals of the grasslands are hoofed animals called ungulates (UHN gyuh lihts). And all ungulates are plant-eaters. Their diet of plants means that they must have grinding teeth. Sharp teeth like those of lions or dogs would be no use for feeding. But without sharp teeth, ungulates still need to defend themselves against predators.

One way to escape an enemy is to run away. The toes of most ungulates became hoofs that are adapted for fast running. Hoofs are made of keratin (KEHR uh tuhn)—the strong, flexible substance that your hair and fingernails are

Giraffe

Hippopotamus

Addax

Axis deer

made of. Odd-toed ungulates, such as zebras and rhinos, have one or three toes on each foot. Even-toed ungulates, such as hippos and giraffes, have two or four toes on each foot.

Another way to defend against predators is to stand and fight. Some ungulates developed sharp horns, which are fearsome weapons. Most horns are growths of bone covered with keratin. Rhino horns are made of hairlike fibers. The horns of buffalo, pronghorn, and antelopes

grow from the forehead. Rhinos' horns grow from the nose.

Deer were the only ungulates to develop antlers, and in most species only males have them. Antlers are not true horns. Both horns and antlers are pointed, bony growths. But horns are covered with hard skin that is rich in keratin, and horns are permanent. Antlers are covered with velvety skin that rubs off over time. Deer shed their antlers every year and then grow new ones.

Zebra

TROPICAL RAIN FOREST ANIMALS

What are tropical rain forests?

The sun shines brightly on the tops of the tallest trees in a tropical rain forest. The raspings of countless insects and the chattering of birds and monkeys fill the hot, wet air. A hungry harpy eagle circles overhead, on the lookout for a capuchin (KAP yoo chihn) monkey, one of its favorite foods. Most animals in a tropical rain forest live in the upper canopy. The trees there are 100 to 150 feet (30 to 45 meters) high, and their leaves are green all year round.

Tropical rain forests

Lower down, on the branch of a shorter tree, hangs a sloth. Its long fur is streaked with green algae that makes its home there. A tamandua (tuh muhn DWAH), a climbing anteater, flicks out its tongue, collecting insects that scurry along the tree branch. A bird-eating spider hunts for prey.

Far below are the animals that live on the forest floor. In this South American rain forest, jaguars, tapirs, and giant anteaters are among the largest. Rodents, lizards, and frogs scurry around the floor, searching for food.

A South American tropical rain forest

All tropical rain forests, like those in North or South America, Africa, or Asia, have two things in common. They lie close to the equator, so they are warm all year round. And they are rainy! Thunderstorms crash through these forests almost every day.

The large leaves in the canopies block the sunlight. They make the forest floor a dark place where few plants can grow. The trees also shed water from "drip tips" that funnel the rain off their leaves, showering the plants and animals below.

Millions of animals live in rain forests. But if you ever walk through one, you will probably hear many more animals than you will see. Monkeys, apes, flying squirrels, anteaters, snakes, insects, and parrots make their homes far above, in the branches of tall trees. With sharp eyes, you might spot fish, including piranhas, in the rivers. What looks like a log or rock might be a turtle or crocodile.

Rain forests have more species of animals than any other place on Earth. But these forests are so large and the vegetation is so dense that many species of such animals as fish, insects, and snakes have yet to be identified.

Piranha (pih RAHN yuh) is a sharp-toothed fish of South America.

Reptiles, amphibians, and fish are part of the teeming life of rain forest rivers and riverbanks.

How are animals adapted to tropical rain forests?

Look! What's that swooping from tree to tree? It can't be a bird—it's not spreading or flapping its wings. It's a squirrel that flies. If you've never seen one like it, that's because this one lives in the tropical rain forest.

Getting around a rain forest is not always easy. Birds and bats can fly. But not all canopy animals have wings. So how do they get around?

Gliders

Some animals in Southeast Asian rain forests can glide through the air like circus stars. That "flying" squirrel is actually a "gliding" squirrel. It has folds of skin between its front and back legs. When it stretches out its legs, the folds act like glider wings.

Some lizards and frogs, and even a few snakes, glide too. Lizards called geckos and flying dragons have folds of skin like flying squirrels. But the flying tree snake just flattens its body, arches its back, and throws itself from tree to tree!

Gliding helps all these animals move around and get food. It also helps them get away from predators.

Gecko (GEHK oh) is a small, harmless lizard that is usually active at night. Its name comes from *gekok*, a word in the Malay language that imitates its cry.

A parachute gecko spreads and flattens its limbs to glide from tree to tree.

Carrying its baby, a three-toed sloth clings to a branch. It uses its long, strong claws to climb and hang.

Climbers

Are you good at climbing trees? Many rain forest animals are experts. Humans use just legs and hands, but these animals have special equipment—long claws and wonderful tails.

Look at the three-toed sloth of South and Central America. Its powerful claws help it climb trees and hang from branches. The sloth's claws are so strong that it can sleep hanging upside down.

A jaguar relaxes on the limb of a rain forest tree in Brazil.

The tamandua is adapted both for climbing and for feeding on the termites and ants that live in rain forest trees.

Other tree-climbers with sharp claws include civets, marmosets, and jaguars. Parrots and parakeets flit between the leaves in the canopy on short wings. Parrots also have strong beaks and claws that help them climb from branch to branch.

The tamandua, a tree-living anteater, has sharp claws and a prehensile (pree HEHNS uhl) tail. It can wrap its tail around a branch and hang from the branch while it searches for food, usually termites and ants.

Many other animals, including spider and howler monkeys, also have prehensile tails. The kinkajou (KIHNG kuh joo), a member of the raccoon family, the tree porcupine, and the woolly opossum use their tails to balance on branches and grasp hard-to-reach fruit and flowers.

Sloth (slawth) is a very slow-moving mammal. Its name comes from an English word that means "laziness."

Civet (SIHV iht) is a fuzzy, catlike mammal.

Marmoset (MAHR muh zeht) is a small species of monkey found only in South America.

Jaguar (JAG wahr)— This animal's name comes from a word that means "it kills with a bound."

A siamang's long arms are adapted for brachiation— swinging through trees with arm-over-arm movements.

Swingers and stickers

Brachiation means moving by grasping and swinging with the arms. *Brachiation* and *bracelet* come from the same Latin word that means "arm."

Siamang (SEE uh mang) is the largest gibbon. The gibbon is the smallest ape.

Some rain forest animals travel by swinging. They use their long arms to propel themselves from tree to tree. This swinging movement is called brachiation (BRAY kee AY shuhn).

These animals use their long fingers to grip and release branches quickly. They also have special shoulder joints that make a half-turn each time the animal swings forward.

The siamang of Southeast Asia covers up to 30 feet (9 meters) with one swing! The chimpanzee, spider monkey, and orangutan also use brachiation to get around.

Other tree-dwelling animals rely on their feet to help them climb. The white-lipped tree frog of Australasia (aw struh LAY zhuh) uses its sticky toes to cling to tree trunks. Iguanas and geckos are tree-climbing lizards with ridged feet. A gecko's feet keep it safely attached to a branch even when it's running upside down!

A chameleon moves slowly, gripping the branches with its tweezer-like feet and its grasping toes. Its left eye points forward, looking for a juicy insect to eat. Its right eye glances behind to check for a snake, bird, or other predator. A dragonfly alights nearby, and the chameleon rocks back and forth and side to side, figuring out the exact distance of this possible meal. Suddenly, in the blink of an eye, the chameleon flicks out its long, sticky tongue and the dragonfly vanishes.

Australasia is the area that includes Australia, New Zealand, and New Guinea, and islands of the South Pacific Ocean.

A tree frog gets a grip on a leaf with its sticky toes.

Getting food and drink

In tropical rain forests, many animals live off the huge supply of plants, including their fruits, seeds, flowers, and leaves. Not surprisingly, animals in tropical rain forests have body parts that are adapted to eat and digest such food.

The hummingbird dines on the nectar (sweet liquid) of brightly colored tropical flowers. Hovering over a blossom, it pokes its thin, curved bill into the flower's deep, narrow center. A perfect fit! The hummingbird sips the nectar.

Toucans (TOO kanz), large beautiful birds with colorful beaks, prefer fruit. They use their long beaks to pluck fruit from trees.

The uakari (wah KAHR ee) monkey, which lives in the Amazon, eats seeds. To get to the tasty meat inside each seed, it uses its sharp teeth, which are just right for cracking open hard shells.

In Africa, the colobus (KAHL uh buhs) monkey can eat leaves that are poisonous. As it digests the leafy fiber, its stomach and liver help it get rid of the harmful substances.

Tapirs (TAY puhrz), which live in Asia and South America, have noses that look like short, fleshy trunks. They use them to sniff out the plants they eat and to pick off the leaves and shoots.

Tapir is a large mammal that is related to the rhino but looks somewhat like a pig.

Flowers, fruit, seeds, leaves, and water plants are all food for animals of the South American rain forest.

Three Honduran white bats roost on a leaf in a forest in Costa Rica.

Raising young safely

In a tropical rain forest, predators are everywhere. Animals have some amazing ways to keep their babies safe.

Several species of tent bat place their young in the large leaves of plants called heliconias (hehl uh KOH nee uhz). The bats chew parts of the leaf to make it curl over their offspring. The young bats are then protected from sun, rain, and predators.

Hornbills make their nest inside a hollow tree. Before the female lays her eggs, she builds a wall with mud, sealing herself inside. This protects her and the chicks from predators. At feeding time, the male sticks fruit or insects on the tip of his large beak and passes them to the female through a slit in the wall.

In some species, the female breaks out when the young are half-grown. The chicks seal the wall, and she then helps to feed them. Other species tear down the wall when the young are strong enough to fly.

The male hornbill feeds the female while she is walled into her nest.

The male strawberry
poison dart frog sits
on the eggs.

Strawberry poison dart frogs of South America
lay their eggs on the forest floor. The male sits on
the eggs.

When the tadpoles hatch, they wriggle onto
their mother's sticky back. She carries them up a
tree and drops them into pools of water in plants.
In these mini-ponds, the tadpoles develop
into frogs.

When the eggs hatch, the
female carries the tadpoles
to water.

Brazil's rain forests are shrinking as more people harvest timber, clear land, and build homes. The little monkeys called golden lion tamarins (TAM uhr ihnz), named for their bright orange fur, have suffered as a result. At one time, they numbered less than a thousand. Keepers at several zoos now raise tamarins and release the captive-born monkeys onto zoo grounds to "train" them to cope with life in the wild. These keepers hope to help the monkeys survive when they are released into protected rain forest homes.

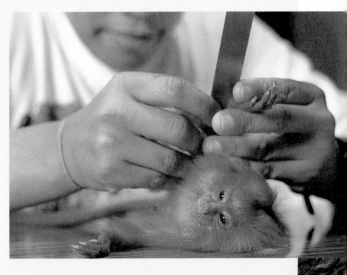

Insects of tropical rain forests

Imagine carrying an object that weighs fifty times more than you do—in your teeth! Humans could never do that, but leaf-cutter (or parasol) ants can.

These amazing ants grow fungus gardens in their nests. They travel long distances in search of certain leaves. When they spot the right leaves, they each cut out a small piece with their sharp mandibles, or jaws. Then they carry the pieces back to their underground nest, holding them over their heads like parasols. They use the leaves to grow their fungus—the only food these ants eat.

In a tropical forest, insects are everywhere—below, on, and above the forest floor. There are termites, mosquitoes, beetles, wasps, bees, fleas, spiders, moths, and butterflies too. Some eat leaves. Some prefer fruit or the nectar of flowers. Some, such as termites, prefer wood, and some, such as the mantis, eat other insects.

Borneo walking stick, life size

A few, such as
female mosquitoes,
drink blood.
   Mosquitoes and
many other insects
lay their eggs in
small pools of
water, often
inside plants.
Some

insects lay their
eggs in underground
nests. And a few lay their eggs
in a host insect.
   Insects can be very small,
like the tiny flea, or very large.
The Borneo walking stick can
grow an incredible 13 inches
(32 centimeters) long. Rain
forest insects also come in
many colors and shapes. The
golden beetle looks like a piece
of gold, while the bull's-eye
silk moth seems to have eyes
on its wings.

Many poisonous insects
are bright-colored. This warns
other animals to watch out.
An animal that gets sick from
eating one of them soon learns
to recognize the bright colors
and avoids that kind of insect.
   So far, about a million
kinds of insects have been
discovered. But scientists
believe there are thousands—
or even millions—of
species yet to be
found.

Can they hide from you?

How many animals can you spot in this picture?
Look carefully—the eight animals can be very hard
to find! When you are finished, turn to page 100.

Hide-and-seek

To avoid their enemies, some animals have developed a way to hide themselves called camouflage (KAM uh flazh) or cryptic (KRIHP tihk) coloration. These animals have a coloring or pattern of markings that makes them look like something else. The animals can blend in with their surroundings, such as a pile of leaves or the bark of a tree. Some, like the chameleon, even change color!

Insects and reptiles are good at blending in. But did you know that the tiger's striped coat and the jaguar's spotted coat are also good camouflage? Even beautiful birds are difficult to spot among the colorful plants—until they start to move.

Did you find all these animals on the previous page?

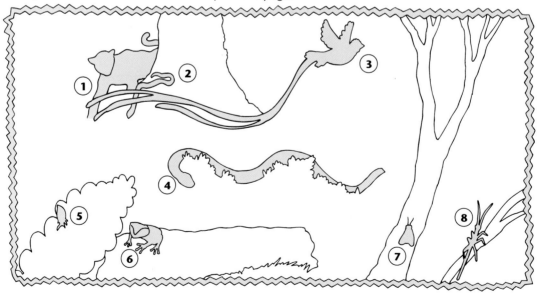

1) Jaguar, 2) Peruvian forest pitviper, 3) Quetzal, 4) Boa constrictor, 5) False-leaf katydid, 6) Horned toad, 7) Tiger moth, 8) American walking stick

Would you . . .?

Would you be an eater of plants?
Or an eater of ants who ate plants?
Or, given your druthers,
Would you really much rather
Be an eater of eaters of ants?

When you moved, would you use
brachiation—
the orangutan's swinging gyration?
Would you slither around,
Crawl through holes in the ground,
Or discover some new transportation?

Would you dress like a leaf or a limb?
Would your coloring help you blend in?
Or would you choose colors
That told all the others,
"Clear a path, stay away, I'm no friend"?

FOREST ANIMALS

What are forests with seasons like?

In the gray light of dawn, a chorus of rising and falling chirping notes, almost like a small orchestra, fills the air of a North American forest. A colony of robins returns from its winter home and perches on branches still wet from the spring rain. Pale green leaves have begun to appear. In twos and threes, the birds flutter to the ground. They hop and stop, looking and listening for bugs and worms in the soil.

Temperate forests

Soon a male and a female pair off and find a nesting place. The male helps build the nest, and the female settles down to hatch her clutch of eggs.

In the heat of summer, when the leaves are heavy and dark, the pair raise their chicks and take turns feeding them.

Brood (brewd) is a group of young birds hatched at one time in the nest or cared for together.

Food is plentiful. The pair forage constantly, adding fruit and berries to their diet.

Before summer is over, the pair raise two or three broods. In spite of the parents' efforts to feed and guard them, not all of the chicks survive. While they are learning to fly, they are easy prey for a fox or a house cat gone wild.

The days grow shorter, and the wind is cold and sharp. Fruits are almost gone, and leaves are falling. The remaining chicks are fully feathered. Most of the other birds have already left when the robins take to the air. They will nest again in warmer woodlands to the south.

A North American forest

105

Deciduous means shedding leaves each year. The word comes from Latin words that mean "to fall away."

Taiga is an evergreen forest. It gets its name from the Russian word for the forest, *tajga*.

American robins, and many other animals, make their home in temperate forests. Temperate forests are woodlands that have changing seasons and many kinds of trees, shrubs, and other plants. The trees are all or mostly deciduous (dih SIHD yoo uhs). Deciduous trees grow new leaves in the spring and shed them in fall.

Where winters are mild, forests of broadleaf trees stay green all year round. These are called temperate evergreen forests.

A taiga—a cold-climate forest of conifers

Lands in colder climates, with short summers and long, hard winters, have vast forests called taiga (TY guh). The forests are needleleaf trees. Needleleaf trees are called conifers because their seeds lie in cones. Almost all conifers are evergreen. They keep their needles all year round.

All forests provide animals with shelter, food, and places to rear their young. And even in cold climates, some animals stay in their forest habitats all year long.

How animals live in forests with seasons

In summer, the deciduous forest is a green paradise. Animals find food and shelter everywhere, from the treetops to the forest floor.

Life on the forest floor

A layer of plant litter—leaves, branches, and fallen tree trunks—covers the forest floor. This moist layer is a rich food source for living things. Mushrooms and other fungi break down the litter, and insects feed on decayed wood and leaves.

Frogs, toads, and lizards eat the insects. Slugs slither and salamanders (SAL uh man duhrz) crawl around the rotting logs. Wood lice breathe through pores in their skin. These animals need moisture from the forest floor. If they dry out, they die.

Small mammals such as mice feed on plants, mushrooms, and invertebrates in the litter. Snakes smell with the tips of their forked tongues. In New Zealand forests, the kiwi (KEE wee) uses its long beak and keen sense of smell to dig for worms.

Like many forest animals, the wild boar has a short, strong body adapted for running through underbrush. Deer and moose live here too. Unlike many deer, the small roe deer have short, straight antlers. In the forest, they can move easily through low-branching trees and bushes and hide from predators. When it is safe, the deer roam to nearby fields to feed.

Break down means "separate into parts." Leaves break down when they decay.

Deer comes from an old English word. At one time, it simply meant "animal."

In and on the branches

Animals in temperate forests, like animals in tropical rain forests, are adapted to living in trees. The forests are full of flying and gliding creatures—birds and insects and even flying squirrels. Woodpeckers use their toes to grip a tree while they bore holes in search of tasty grubs. Later, other animals, such as owls, bats, or squirrels, may use the hole as their home.

Koalas use the first two toes of their front paws like thumbs to grip branches as they climb. Black bears use their claws to dig up bulbs, grasp prey, and grab honey. Bears also use their claws to scratch trees to mark their territory. Opossums wrap their hairless tails around branches to climb or feed—or just hang upside down.

Speaking of tails, have you ever seen tightrope-walkers carry a pole to keep their balance? Some animals do this. For example, a squirrel uses its long tail for balance.

Opossums are named for their pale color. The name comes from an American Indian word that means "white animal."

Camouflage comes from a French word that means "disguise."

Other tree dwellers have camouflage that protects them from predators. Many insects have the same color and shape as leaves or sticks. Walking sticks, for example, look just like twigs. Some treehoppers look like thorns. And katydids look like leaves to predators.

Opossum

Red-bellied woodpecker

Forest waterholes

Moose is from a Native American word that means "twig eater."

The lakes and rivers of forests are home to many creatures. Moose feed on land, but they also wade in rivers and lakes to eat water lilies and other plants. They need the plants' valuable nutrients. Raccoons use their forepaws to feel in the shallow waters for crayfish, frogs, and other tasty foods.

For water birds, lakes and rivers are places to feed, shelter, and raise young. Grebes (greebz) are built for water life. Their toe and ankle joints are so flexible that they can turn their feet in all directions to paddle, steer, or dive.

Grebes feed on insects, fish, and mollusks. In spring, after

This moose is grazing on water plants, an important part of its diet.

courting, a pair build a floating island of plants fastened to a living plant. There they nest and raise their chicks through the summer. Loons also nest away from shore. They build on islands, stone outcroppings, or even logs.

A beaver builds its lodge from tree branches.

Beavers are excellent swimmers. Their lodges have underwater entrances that are hard for other animals to reach. In the fall, as freezing weather begins, the beavers coat their lodges with mud. The frozen mud keeps the lodges warm and is almost impossible for predators to break.

Grebes' legs and feet are built for swimming and diving.

Gearing up for winter

In winter, food is harder to find in temperate forests. Trees lose leaves and fruit, and snow often covers the ground. Animals get ready for winter.

Some forest birds migrate—travel to a warmer place. Many snakes, bats, and rodents hibernate. Their temperature falls, their heartbeat and breathing slow down, and they sleep through the winter in a burrow or nest. Bears, skunks, and some other animals

ACORN
VENDING
MACHINE

EXACT
CHANGE
ONLY

sleep most of the winter, waking up only now and then. But some animals stay awake and manage to survive.

Many animals store up food for the winter. They gather nuts, seeds, bulbs, and grasses. To defend their supply, the acorn woodpeckers make their own vending machine! They hammer holes in a dead tree and pop an acorn into each hole. When they get hungry, they know where to peck.

Some animals have learned to keep food from spoiling. Red squirrels dry mushrooms on a branch before they hide them. Other animals store live food. Moles give earthworms a bite that makes them unable to move. They store the worms in a safe place and dine on fresh worms all winter long.

Braving the winter

Some animals adapt to winter conditions by changing their diet. For example, moose and deer nibble on twigs and tree bark in winter, when green plants are scarce. They also use the trees as protection from the harsh winter cold and winds.

Other animals are highly adapted to life with snow. Many mammals grow a thicker coat of fur to help them stay warm. Some even have a thick furry tail that they wrap around themselves for extra warmth.

A few small rodents, such as voles (vohlz) and shrews, spend the winter in snow tunnels near the ground. These snow tunnels are made of ice crystals. The tunnels form when heat from the ground melts the first layers of snow. When more snow falls, the tunnels remain. The layers of deep snow trap heat from the ground, so it never gets too cold in the tunnels.

Reindeer roam the Siberian taiga.

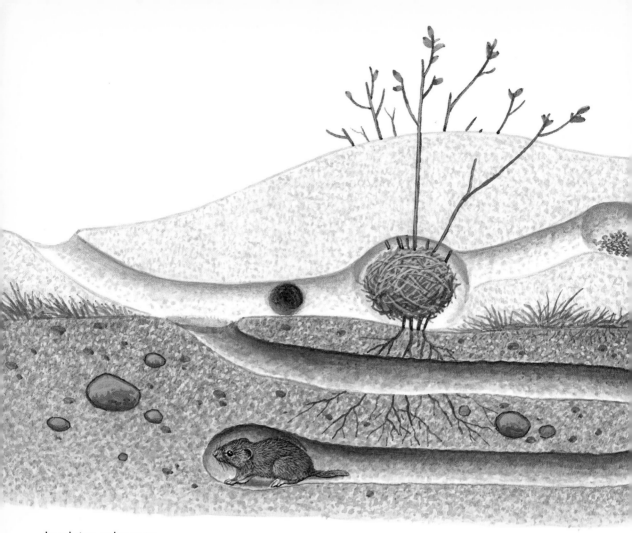

In winter, voles may tunnel underground or through packed snow to find and store food.

Snow tunnels protect small mammals from predators as well as from the cold. Snow tunnels also help them find food easily and store it. Voles store piles of grasses in their tunnels, but they also feed by burrowing. In winter, they dig for roots. When the snow is deep enough to cover bushes, one kind of vole digs for berries that birds can no longer reach. Another kind of vole stands on packed snow to browse on shrubs that it can't reach during the summer.

HELPING HANDS

People love cuddly koalas. Most zoos that have koalas have koala breeding programs, but there aren't enough of the animals for all the zoos that want them. In Australia, where koalas live in the forests, some zoos may be tempted to replenish their collections with wild koalas, which is against the law. So police in Australia record the fingerprints of all "legal" zoo koalas. A captive koala whose fingerprints don't match police records won't get arrested–but someone who sells or buys a wild koala might!

Which season is it?

Forest animals know what season it is—whether it is time to build a nest, play, prepare for winter, or survive the harsh cold. They take their cues from Mother Nature. Match each animal activity shown on page 121 with the season in which it takes place in the temperate forest.

SPRING

SUMMER

AUTUMN

WINTER

1.

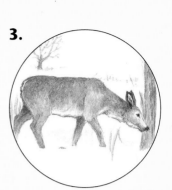

Bear eating honey

2.

Grebe with chick

3.

Deer nibbling bark

4.

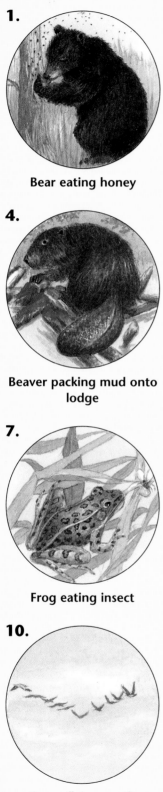

Beaver packing mud onto
lodge

5.

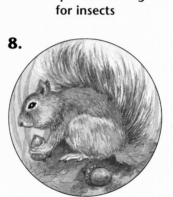

Woodpecker looking
for insects

6.

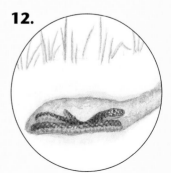

Bear walking
with cubs

7.

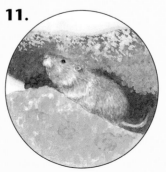

Frog eating insect

8.

Squirrel gathering nuts

9.

Grebe building nest

10.

Geese flying south

11.

Vole nibbling
stored berries

12.

Snake sleeping
in burrow

Snow monkeys of Japan

Most apes and monkeys live in tropical climates—but not the snow monkey, or Japanese macaque (muh KAHK). This hardy monkey does quite well in the harsh winters of northern Japan.

The Japanese macaque is a large monkey with a short tail. The skin on its face is a reddish-pink. That's why it's also called the red-faced macaque.

Unlike their tropical cousins, Japanese macaques have had to adapt to freezing cold winters. First of all, they eat a variety of foods. So they can always find something good to eat—even when the ground is covered with snow.

In summer, Japanese macaques eat leaves, seeds, grasses, insects, mushrooms, eggs, seaweed, crabs, and their favorite foods—fruits, berries, and nuts. In winter, when these foods are not available, they make do on a diet of buds and bark.

Keeping warm is not easy either. Japanese macaques have thick, shaggy coats. They also use the buddy system to keep the cold out. Groups of these monkeys huddle together for warmth in trees on a hillside that is protected from the wind. But these monkeys have found an even better way to escape the cold—they take a hot bath!

In the far northern mountains, where some Japanese macaques live, there are many natural hot springs. Hot springs form where melted rock, called magma, lies closer than usual to the earth's surface. The magma heats up underground water, which then bubbles up to form hot springs, or pools.

When macaques need a break from the snow and ice, they get into the warm water and soak. They often sit there for hours, with only their heads above the water. When they get out, they shake off the water and face the cold again. Their thick fur coats keep them from catching a chill.

Now, is that a cool monkey or what?

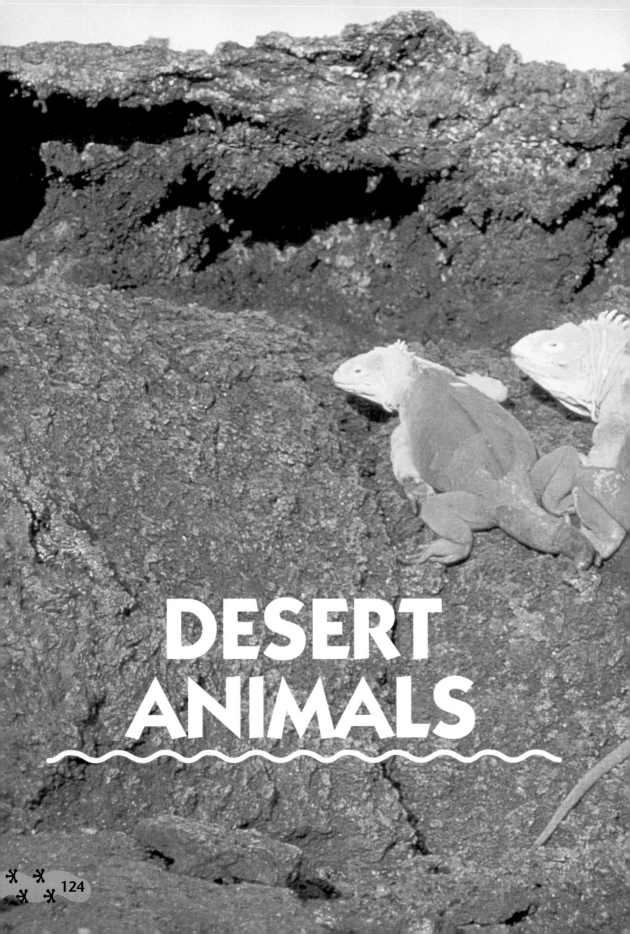

DESERT
ANIMALS

What are desert homes like?

The tiny fox called a fennec (FEHN ehk) crouches against a ridge of sand, watching for a jerboa (juhr BOH uh), a little mouselike animal. The fennec's pale fur blends with the sand. Its large ears help it throw off heat by day and hear its tiny prey at night, when it hunts.

Deserts

The jerboa sneaks out of its warm burrow on this chilly desert evening. It tries to forage for small seeds and shoots. A jerboa doesn't need to drink water because its body makes water from the food it eats.

The fennec and the jerboa live in the Sahara, the world's largest desert. Temperatures there may reach more than 110 °F (43 °C) by day. But not all deserts are hot. There are cold deserts, such as the Gobi Desert of northern China, for example, where winter temperatures average only 10 °F (-12 °C), and summer temperatures are about 70 °F (21 °C). In cold deserts, some jerboas hibernate in winter. And deserts are not always vast stretches of sand either. Some deserts, such as the Great Salt Lake Desert in Utah, are covered with bare rock, loose stone, clay, and salty soil.

Jerboa comes from the Arabic word for the animal, "yarbu´."

127

Do not be fooled by an empty-looking desert. Every desert has some living things. Even the hottest and coldest deserts are home to at least a few kinds of plants and animals. But all deserts have one thing in common—they are dry! Their plants and animals must get along on very little water. Because deserts can be very hot or cold, plants and animals must be able to handle extreme temperatures.

This rabbit-eared bandicoot kicks sand at the face of a snake— a defense that gives it time to run for its burrow.

Many desert animals burrow for shelter. They may dig temporary holes to hide in while they are foraging, or build permanent burrows to raise their young. Large plants, such as cactuses, also provide homes for some animals. In the Southwestern United States, woodpeckers and owls nest in holes in the thick stems of cactuses.

Many insects and spiders live in the desert. They make juicy meals for birds and lizards. Jerboas and grasshopper mice eat insects too, but most small desert mammals eat plants.

In turn, the small plant-eaters are food for meat-eating animals, such as foxes, snakes, and birds. Larger animals with hoofs, such as gazelles and camels, also live in deserts. They eat tough desert plants.

How do animals live in deserts?

Desert animals must keep cool when the desert is hot and warm when it's cold. They need food, and their bodies need water, which is scarce.

To handle heat and cold, some animals stay in the shade or burrow underground. Many look for food only at dusk or dawn.

Gambel's quail

Collared lizard

MORNING

DAYTIME A Northern flicker finds a cool and shaded place to rest inside a saguaro cactus.

EVENING After the hot sun begins to set, a praying mantis grabs its meal.

Lizards are cold-blooded. On cool desert mornings, they soak in the warmth of the sun to become active. Later in the day, they may shelter in the shade.

NIGHTTIME A furry coat keeps this cat warm while it hunts during the cold desert night.

131

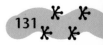

Getting water

Insects, spiders, scorpions, and their relatives look dressed for the desert. These little creatures have hard outer bodies made out of chitin (KY tihn). Chitin is waterproof. It keeps water inside their bodies, so they don't dry out.

A small snake is a meal for this imperial scorpion.

Scorpions get all the water they need from eating insects, spiders, and lizards. First a scorpion stings another animal so that it cannot move. Then the scorpion chews its prey to mush and sucks it in.

Desert spiders never spin webs to catch insects—that would take too much water. Instead, they stalk their prey or hide behind rocks and pounce on it. The larger spiders hunt lizards too, and even small birds.

Some honeypot ants store food in

their bodies! These ants love sap from plants, called honeydew. Some ants gather the honeydew and feed it to "storage" ants, who eat so much they swell up. They hang from the roof of their nest, full of honeydew, until the other ants need food. Then the storage ants spit up the honeydew, drop by drop.

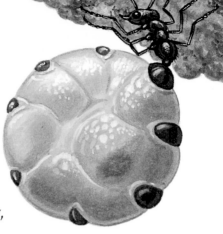

Storage ants like this one hold the honeydew for a colony of honeypot ants.

Darkling beetles get water in a most unusual way. On foggy days, which are common in their home, the Namib Desert of Africa, the beetles stand on their heads. The fog cools on their bodies, turns into water, and trickles right into their mouths.

A headstand gives this darkling beetle a drink. Droplets of water roll down its body and into its mouth.

The thorny devil hunts a meal of ants in the heat of day. At night, it drinks dew that forms on its body.

Lizards also do well in the desert. Their scaly skin holds in water. And their urine contains so little water that it's almost solid!

The thorny devil eats about 7,000 ants a day! During the cold night, dew forms on the thorny devil's body. Tiny grooves in the animal's skin bring the dew to its mouth.

Snakes, including poisonous vipers, live in every desert. Some vipers bury themselves in sand until another animal comes along. Then they strike! One meal can keep a snake satisfied for weeks.

Even large animals can survive the dryness. The oryx (OHR ihks) of Africa and Asia drink by licking dew off each other. They can get as hot as 116 °F (47 °C) without overheating! Most of the time, a camel gets enough moisture from the tough plants it eats. When food is scarce, it lives on the "energy pack" of fat stored in its hump.

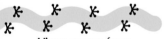

Viper comes from Latin words that mean "live-bearing." Most kinds of snakes lay eggs, but almost all true vipers give birth to live young.

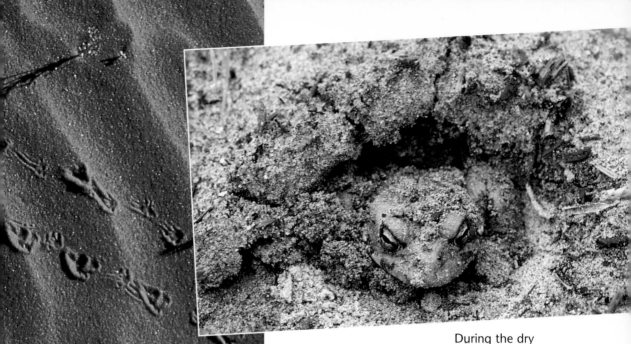

During the dry
season, a desert toad
shelters in its burrow.

Some animals need to wait until there is enough water to have babies. Desert toads sleep in burrows until the rainy season arrives. After it rains, they lay eggs in puddles.

The male sand grouse takes a swim each day, but not to cool off. Every day, it flies to a water hole— sometimes as far as 22 miles (35 kilometers) away. While there, it splashes its entire body. Its soft breast feathers become soaked like a sponge. Then the bird flies all the way back to its young, carrying water for them to drink from its feathers.

Male sand grouse

Camel spiders

Do you know which desert animal has the fiercest bite for its size? It's the camel spider, also known as the sun spider. Camel spiders live in deserts everywhere in the world except Australia.

A camel spider's bite isn't poisonous. But many people are scared of camel spiders because they are so hairy, so huge, and so hungry! Hairs cover their body, especially their eight legs. Camel spiders touch things with these hairs.

These animals grow almost 3 inches (7.6 centimeters) long and attack any prey they find. They usually dine on large grasshoppers, beetles, spiders, and termites, but some eat lizards, small birds, and rodents (animals like rats and mice).

For their size, camel spiders have the strongest "jaws" of any animal. Actually, these aren't real jaws. They are two hollow parts, called *chelicerae* (kuh LIHS uh ruh), that look like legs. Camel spiders use them to grab their prey. Then they suck out its body fluids to get food and water.

Camel spiders aren't real spiders, but they are related. They are a group called *solifugae* (sah LIHF yoo gay), which means "fleeing from the sun."

Most camel spiders live in burrows and come out at night to hunt. Female camel spiders are especially keen hunters. They run in zigzags, searching for food in burrows, under

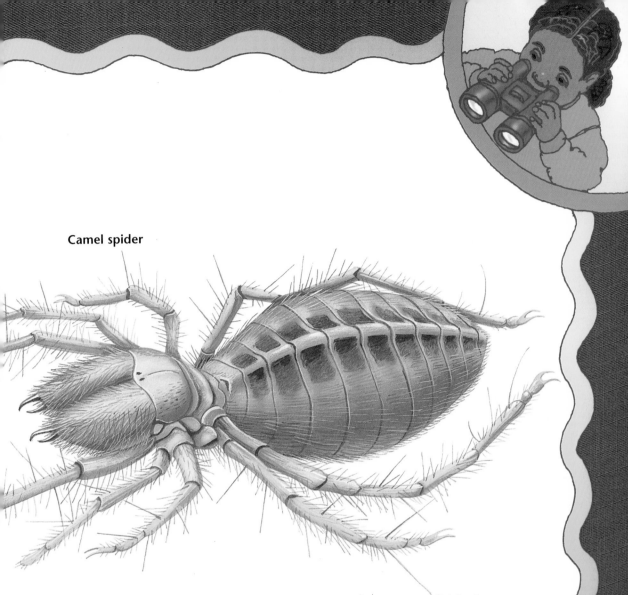

Camel spider

rocks, and in grass. One kind even climbs trees, using special suckers on its legs.

No one is sure how camel spiders know where other animals are hiding. They may use smell.

One kind of camel spider, which lives in the Namib Desert of Africa, digs up grasshoppers that are hiding in the sand. How can it tell where the grasshoppers are? Maybe its hairs sense the grasshoppers' movement.

Once camel spiders find their prey, the chase begins. Camel spiders can move as fast as 10 miles (16 kilometers) an hour. Of all land animals without a backbone, they are probably the fastest.

Cool ideas

Your body cools off by sweating, but many desert animals cool off in other ways. Birds, such as ostriches, hold up their feathers to let the air cool their skin. A bird's body temperature is high—about 104 °F (40 °C)—so it doesn't overheat easily.

In the desert, birds also stay cool by nesting in the shade—in bushes, rocks, and burrows. Some even build mounds of pebbles to shade their nests. And some, such as coursers, stand over their nests to shade their chicks.

Lizards hide from the scorching heat beneath the sand or a rock. Their bodies can't control their temperature. If the ground is hot, you may see a lizard in a special pose—with one of its front legs, one of its back legs, and its belly off the ground.

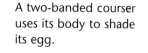

A two-banded courser uses its body to shade its egg.

A jack rabbit raises its ears to keep cool. The blood circulating through its large, thin ears gives off heat from its body.

Severe heat and cold are most dangerous to small mammals. For example, because a mouse is much smaller than a camel, it warms up and cools down more quickly. During cold nights or hot days, it could freeze or cook!

Many small mammals avoid this fate by burrowing under the sand. Jerboas, which are related to mice, live in Africa and Asia. Some kinds leave their burrows only at night. Naked mole rats of the Sahara never leave their burrows. They dig for roots and bulbs underground.

Animals that are too big to dig burrows lie in the shade. Gazelles look for the shade of rocks or plants. Jack rabbits scratch out cool pockets in the sand. They also can raise their huge ears to draw heat out of their bodies. At night, however, they wrap their ears around their body to keep warm.

Jack rabbits are really hares—but they are closely related to rabbits. Unlike rabbits, hares don't burrow. Also, baby hares are born with fur and with their eyes open. Baby rabbits are born naked and with their eyes closed.

139

The quokka (KWAH kuh) of Australia looks like a small kangaroo. It keeps cool by licking its feet, tail, and belly. Where does it get enough water to do all this licking?

Wild cats (such as the lynx) and dogs (such as the dingo) stay cool by panting. Panting uses up their water, so these animals usually live near water holes that are filled by underground springs or by sudden rainstorms.

Camels hardly sweat at all. Instead, their body temperature safely rises several degrees by day and falls at night. Have you ever wondered why there is a hump of fat on a camel's back? Well, consider how hot the camel would be if the fat were evenly spread out all over its body. It would have a layer of fatty insulation, just like a bear or seal. However, camels don't need that insulation in a hot desert!

Camels' bodies are adapted to desert life. Thick eyelashes keep out blowing sand and shade the eyes. Wide feet spread to help them stay on top of shifting sands. And between meals, they live off the fat stored in their humps.

HELPING HANDS

The nomadic Rendille people of Kenya, who herd livestock, have shared their desert home with gerenuk and oryx for thousands of years. When the government ordered the Rendille to stop migrating with their cattle, goats, and camels and stay in one place, the result was disaster. Their animals ate all the green plants, which could not grow back fast enough to provide adequate food. The Rendille, their animals, and the gerenuk and oryx suffered. Soon, the government realized that the nomadic life was more in balance with the desert and let the Rendille return to their ancient lifestyle.

Cave animals

In some parts of the desert, animals don't have to worry about thirst, cold, or heat. These animals live in a cool, dark world—caves.

Caves are found in many deserts. For example, Australia's Ayers Rock (called *Uluru* in Aboriginal) is surrounded by desert and has many small caves. But for animals, life inside a cave is nothing like life outside. A cave is a different habitat, another world.

Caves are dark and quiet. They never get very cold or very hot. Caves are damp, too. Many have underground lakes, rivers, and waterfalls. Because caves are dark, no green plants grow there. But many animals live in caves.

Sometimes winds or floods carry in food, such as twigs or pollen, that feed cockroaches and beetles. These insects are eaten by spiders, fish, and by other insects. Bats and birds, such as swiftlets, eat insects too. Many insects, such as flies and earwigs, eat bat droppings. Bacteria and fungi, which don't need light to survive, grow on droppings and other wastes.

Many cave-dwelling animals are related to animals outside, but their bodies have changed to help them survive in caves. Because caves are dark, the animals don't need protective coloring. Many have no color at all. Cave beetles are white. Salamanders and cavefish look pink because they are so pale that their blood shows through their flesh!

In the dark, sight is useless. Some cave animals, such as shrimp and crabs, have small eyes. And some, such as cavefish, are blind. Other senses, like touch, are more important in caves. Some insects, such as crickets, feel

their way around with
extremely long antennae (an
TEHN ee). Bats and swiftlets
rely on echoes.

Many cave animals need to
search in tiny spaces for food.
So most cave animals are small.
Some cavefish are only about
4/5 inch (2 centimeters) long—
only half as big as their cousins
aboveground!

Cavefish is the name of just one
family of cave-dwelling fish in the
United States. More than 20 other
kinds of blind fish live in caves or in
the deep sea.

A desert tale

The skin of the thorny devil, a lizard that lives in Australia, is blotchy and covered with spines. It looks so ugly, it is no surprise that its scientific name is *Moloch horridus*. The word *moloch* comes from the name of an ancient devil god. The word *horridus* speaks for itself!

Many desert animals avoid the thorny devil, because it looks so scary. In fact, it is harmless. When the thorny devil is frightened, it tucks its head between its legs! This Australian folk tale explains how the thorny devil got its thorns—and its name.

One day a lizard was playing with a boomerang. He loved throwing the wooden toy. No matter how far it flew, it always came back.

As the lizard was playing, a cockatoo flew down to watch. The lizard knew the cockatoo was watching. He was a show-off, and he hoped she was admiring his skill.

The lizard's throws became fancier and fancier—too fancy. Something went wrong. Instead of returning to him, the boomerang slammed into the cockatoo's head and knocked off most of her lovely head feathers. Only a few remained, standing in a kind of crest.

"You idiot!" shrieked the cockatoo. "I'll get you for that."

The lizard tried to run and hide. But he was too scared to think straight. He ran toward a thorn-covered bush. The cockatoo grabbed the lizard in her claws and shoved the unfortunate animal into the thorns.

"That'll teach you to show off!"
cried the cockatoo.

Try as he might, the lizard couldn't
get those thorns out. Ever since, he's
been called a "thorny devil." As for
the cockatoo, she still has a crest
of feathers on her head.

147

POLAR
ANIMALS

What are polar homes like?

The wind howls. Offshore, the pack ice heaves and crashes, booming like distant thunder. But in her den, deep in a snowbank near the shore, the female polar bear stays warm. Her body heat keeps the temperature just at freezing. Her waterproof coat and a thick layer of fat protect her from the cold.

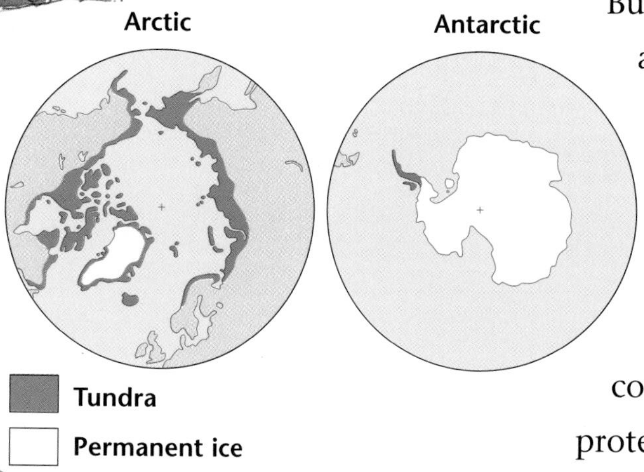

In late November, the Arctic winter is already bitterly cold. But the polar bear isn't hibernating. She is waiting for her young to be born. While she waits, she lives off her fat and mouthfuls of snow.

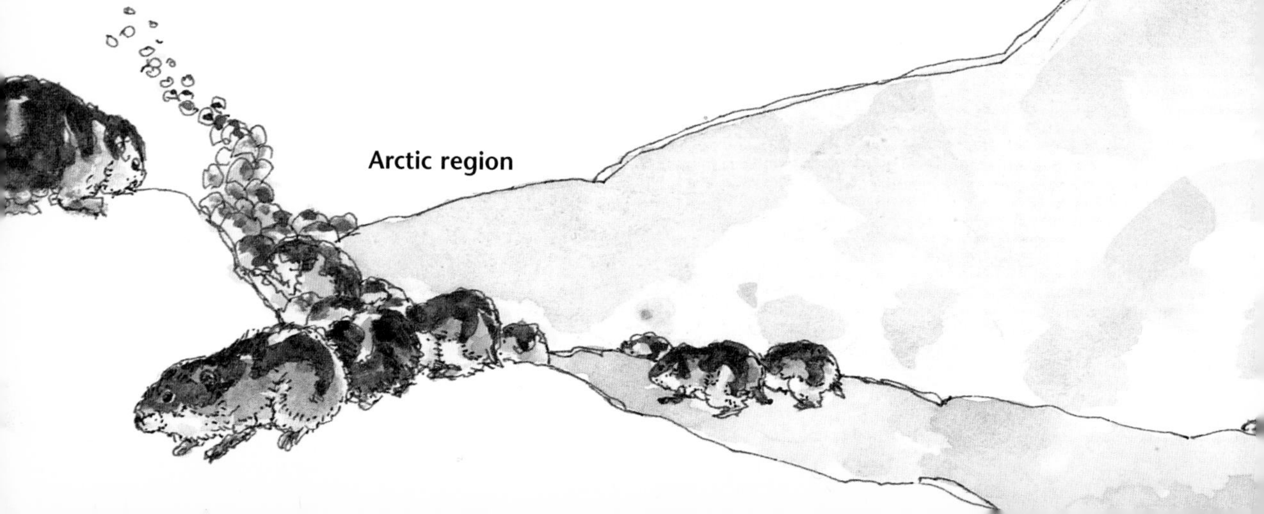

Arctic

Antarctic

Tundra

Permanent ice

Arctic region

Like most mother polar bears, she has twin cubs. When they are born, they will be unable to see, hear, walk, or smell. They will live on their mother's milk, which is rich in fat and protein. By late spring, they will be ready to venture outside.

The polar bear gets its name from the extremely cold climate of its habitat. There are two

Antarctic region

polar regions in the world. The "top" region, around the North Pole, is the Arctic, where polar bears live. At the center is the Arctic Ocean. Around the ocean lie Greenland and the Arctic lands of Europe, Asia, and North America.

The "bottom" region, centered around the South Pole, is the Antarctic. The South Pole is on land— the continent of Antarctica. Around Antarctica lies the Antarctic Ocean.

In the northernmost Arctic, thick sea ice covers most of the ocean all year, and a cap of freshwater ice covers the land. Each summer, icebergs split off the icecap and float into the ocean.

The timber line runs through most of the Arctic lands. Beyond it, the climate is too harsh for trees to grow. North of the timber line lies land called tundra

(TUHN druh). Its shallow surface of rocky soil is ice-free by July, but the ground below it is always frozen. This frozen ground is called permafrost.

On the tundra, plantlike lichens grow in cracks and crevices, pushing apart rocks and breaking them up into soil. Shrubs, mosses, grass, and flowers also grow on the tundra. Plant-eaters such as lemmings feed on the plants. They, in turn, attract meat-eaters such as arctic foxes.

A thick icecap covers Antarctica and extends over Antarctica's bays, forming ice shelves. In summer, flat-topped icebergs split off the shelves.

Few animals live inland on Antarctica, but small, shrimplike krill are plentiful in the waters. They attract seals, penguins, and other krill-loving animals to the Antarctic shores.

153

How do animals live in polar habitats?

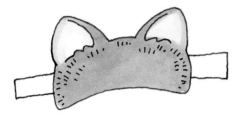 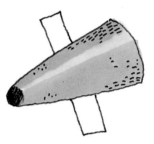

Imagine that you have a job designing things. Your latest assignment is a real challenge: Design an animal that stays warm in polar habitats. How do you begin?

Kit fox

Arctic fox

Rounder means warmer

Try comparing animals in polar regions with animals in warmer areas. For example, foxes, hares, and lemmings in the Arctic have rounder bodies than their cousins in the temperate zone. The polar animals also have shorter ears, noses, legs, and tails.

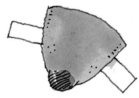

These differences help explain how animals in polar regions stay warm. To understand why, compare an animal and its body heat to a bowl of hot soup. Soup cools faster on a shallow plate than in a bowl because more of the soup's surface is exposed to air. So the soup loses heat quickly. In a bowl, less of the soup's surface is exposed, so the soup stays warm longer.

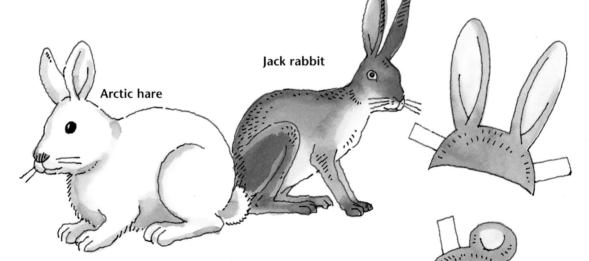

Arctic hare

Jack rabbit

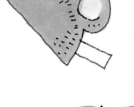

Like the plate, the longer bodies of temperate-zone animals have a larger surface area. The round, stocky bodies of polar animals expose less of their surface. So a round shape and short body parts conserve, or save, body heat.

Order up some fat and fur

Your animal now has a shape. But what materials are best to use? To find out, study the Arctic and Antarctic animals pictured here. What do they all share? One answer is fat. Fat makes great insulation—it provides protection from heat loss.

If you want to make a mammal, it also needs fur or hair. One square inch (6.5 square centimeters) of a fur seal's hide has more than 8,000 fibers. A musk ox has a layer of 3-foot (91-centimeter)-long hair over a layer of short fur.

Polar bears and reindeer, also known as caribou, have

Reindeer are tame caribou. For thousands of years, people in Europe and Asia have herded these animals for meat, hides, transportation, and even medicine.

double-layer coats, too. Hollow guard hairs make up the outer layer. Dense fur, double layers, and hollow hairs all serve the same purpose: they trap and heat air. Warm air is excellent insulation.

A double layer of fur—and close company—keep these musk oxen warm.

The polar bear's fur also acts as a solar heater. Its outer guard hairs look white because they reflect sunlight. They are actually clear. These clear hairs collect the sun's heat like the glass in a greenhouse. The hollow hairs channel the heat to the bear's skin, which is black. And black soaks up heat like a sponge soaks up water.

Dense fur keeps a Siberian tiger (left) warm through cold Arctic winters.

The black back feathers of the dovekie absorb heat from the sun.

Make it waterproof and dark

The fur on most polar mammals is waterproof. For example, wolverine fur sheds water and never freezes. That is why Inuits—Arctic people—use wolverine fur to line parka hoods.

If you plan to create a polar bird, it needs waterproof feathers. You might want to give it a three-layer waterproof coat of short thick feathers, like penguins have. In the Antarctic, this thick coat acts like the fur on mammals. It keeps water out and keeps heat in. In addition, the black feathers on a penguin's back absorb heat from the sun. In the Arctic, the black feathers on dovekies (DUHV keez) and Atlantic puffins do the same job.

You might also want to supply your bird with oil! Most birds care for their feathers by stroking them with oil. The oil comes from a gland at the base of the bird's tail. Water birds have very efficient oil glands that help them keep their feathers waterproof and flexible.

Polar regions certainly have a variety of well-adapted animals! Let's enjoy learning more about the ones that already exist.

Puffins "fly" after fish. Oil keeps their feathers flexible as they beat their wings underwater.

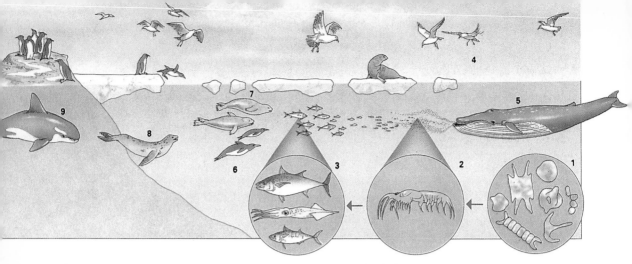

Polar oceans are rich in food. Tiny plankton (1) are eaten by krill (2), which are food for fish (3), birds (4), and fin whales (5). Fish, in turn, are food for penguins (6) and seals (7). Both seals and penguins are eaten by leopard seals (8). And seals, penguins, and smaller whales are eaten by killer whales (9).

Ocean of food

With all that ice in the polar regions, where do you suppose polar animals get their food? Many polar animals rely on the ocean to supply their food throughout the year.

Polar bears can smell a ringed seal 20 miles (32 kilometers) away, and will gladly travel that far for one of their preferred foods. But why would a seal live where there are seal-eating bears? The answer is—algae (AL jee). These tiny plants attract arctic cod, and the fish in turn attract seals and sea birds.

Some sea birds are designed for fishing. Many gulls and skuas (SKYOO uhz) have white undersides, so fish swimming below can hardly see them stalking. Their white bellies blend in with the sky.

Other birds prefer insects to fish. In summer, melted snow turns the tundra into swampland and billions of insects appear. Plovers (PLUHV uhrz) walk along the shore or search in damp areas for insects, beetles, worms, and crustaceans.

Parasitic jaeger

Lemmings, musk oxen, and other plant-eaters live on grass and shrubs on the summer tundra. In winter, caribou use their large hoofs to dig through snow for lichens. Unlike most birds, ptarmigans (TAHR muh guhnz) live in the Arctic all year. These chickenlike birds survive almost entirely on twigs during the long winters.

In the Arctic, small meat-eaters include snowy owls, arctic foxes, and jaegers. They are hunted by wolves, and in summer, by grizzlies and polar bears. However, they often follow wolves and bears—at a safe distance—to feed on their leftovers.

Jaeger (YAY guhr) comes from a German word that means "hunter."

For Emperor and Adélie penguins in Antarctica, mealtime is simple. They dive for krill. But leopard seals hunt swimming penguins, though they seldom bother penguins on ice or land.

Willow ptarmigan

Babies year-round

Choose any month in the year. You are sure to find animals mating, giving birth, or raising young in a polar region.

January—the Antarctic summer— is when leopard seals give birth to their pups. Other kinds of seals give birth in colonies, or groups. But leopard seals give birth alone. Their newborn pups generally weigh as much as a 5-year-old child!

In March, male arctic hares, or jacks, fight over a female, or doe. The doe mates with the winner. By late spring, she produces one to nine leverets (LEHV uhr ihts), or babies.

Arctic foxes live in pairs. They dig a burrow in the side of a hill to shelter their family from the cold. Between May and July, the female gives birth to the cubs, and both parents care for the young. By fall, the cubs have learned to hunt and to care for themselves.

A mother leopard seal
cares for her pup in an
ice den.

These arctic hares are fighting over the territories they control.
In mating season, they fight over females.

Fox cubs venture out of their den during the Arctic summer.
Playing and exploring help them learn hunting skills.

In August, most young snow geese are 1 month old. They have spent their entire short life with their parents and thousands of other geese on the tundra. Now they are ready to fly south.

In November, even the Arctic waters are warmer than the bitterly cold air. A pregnant polar bear digs a den in the snow. She moves in and stays much warmer in her snow cave than she would have outside. In December, her pint-sized twins are born. By early spring, they leave the den to practice belly slides on the Arctic slopes.

 HELPING HANDS

The mighty polar bear is a popular zoo animal, but it's also popular in its natural Arctic habitat—for hunting! People have hunted polar bears, not only for meat but for sport, until there aren't many left. Some bears are safe in zoos, where keepers provide them with many stimulating activities that let them act naturally. As a bonus, zoo visitors learn to appreciate those natural behaviors—and may one day support new laws and other efforts to help the polar bears still living in the wild.

Where Arctic animals

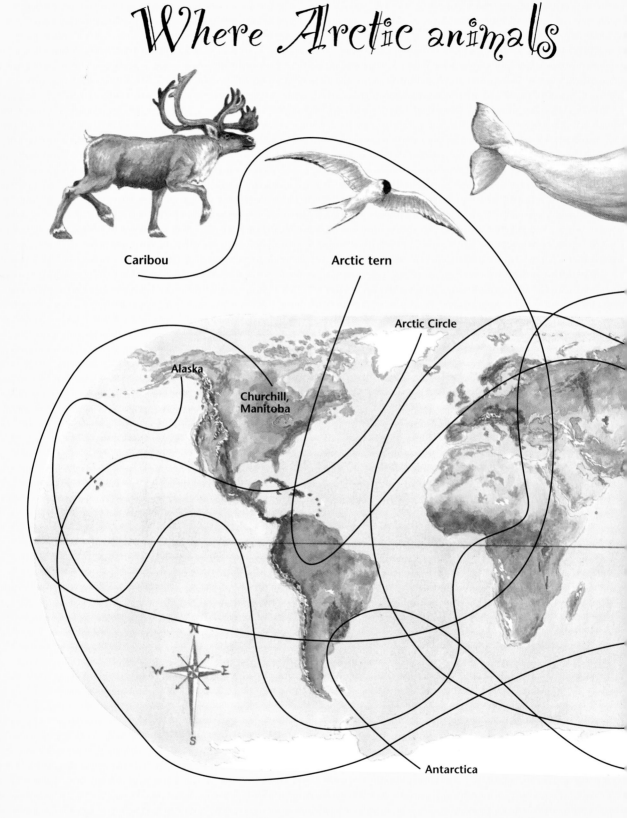

Caribou

Arctic tern

Arctic Circle

Alaska

Churchill,
Manitoba

Antarctica

go during winter

Beluga whale   **Polar bear**   **Snow goose**

When winter comes, many plants die or go dormant till the spring. So food becomes scarce for plant-eaters. If the plant-eaters die, or leave to search for food, the meat-eaters may starve.

The ground squirrel is the only true hibernator in polar regions.

Larger polar animals cannot store enough fat during the summer to get them through the winter.

Animals that cannot live year-round in a polar region usually migrate, or leave, during the winter. Many kinds of birds fly to warmer climates as soon as the young birds mature.

Birds are not the only winter refugees, however. The tundra cannot supply caribou with enough grazing during the winter. So caribou herds migrate south across the timber line and spend the winter in forests. Even polar bears move in winter. They abandon the tundra for the newly frozen sea ice.

These pages show five animals and where they go when freezing winds blow in the Arctic. Where do you think each animal spends the winter? Follow the line from each to a winter home and see if you are correct! For the polar bear, find the town it visits before trekking to a really "cool" winter home. (Of course, real migration routes are more direct than these!)

Japan

167

Wolves

At one time, wolves inhabited the whole northern half of the globe. But for centuries, people relentlessly killed them. Now most wolves live on the tundra or just south of it, below the timber line, or in other areas—from forest to semidesert—where there are few people.

In North America, the wolves south of the timber line are timber wolves. Their fur is gray, brown, black, or a mix of colors. Their keen senses help them find prey. A timber wolf can see and smell a deer 1 mile (1.6 kilometers) away.

Despite their name, timber wolves dislike dense forests. They prefer open spaces where moose and elk are easy to track. Like most wolves, they hunt prey larger than themselves. They do this by working in packs.

The wolves on the tundra are arctic wolves.

They grow long, thick fur that keeps them warm in below-zero temperatures. Even their pale-colored coats help them survive. The wolves can sneak close to prey unseen because their coats blend with the snow.

Arctic wolves need to use their keen senses even more than timber wolves. For almost five months, the Arctic has no

Once they have stalked their game long enough to get close, arctic wolves like these chase down their prey.

sunlight. The wolves must locate their prey in the dark.

Food is scarce on the tundra. Arctic wolves often go for a week or more without eating. When they finally make a kill, they often leave nothing behind. They even eat the fur and bones of lemmings and hares. But wolves would rather feed on larger game, such as caribou and musk oxen, which provide more food for the pack.

Herds of caribou and musk oxen must graze a large area to get enough grass and other plants to survive. Close behind them comes the wolf pack. The wolves sometimes travel hundreds of miles to catch up with their favorite prey.

The pack circles the herd and tries to scatter the animals. Then the wolves separate the old, sick, and young from the rest. These are easiest to kill. One musk ox feeds a pack for a week. The wolves might even leave scraps for ravens and other scavengers.

OCEAN
ANIMALS

What is home like in the ocean?

In the South Pacific Ocean, a huge right whale cruises along the surface. A screen of thin, bony plates called baleen (buh LEEN) hangs from the upper jaw of its half-open mouth. The baleen strains tiny living things from the water pouring through the whale's jaws.

In the frigid waters of the North Atlantic Ocean, a sperm whale lolls on the surface, resting. It has just made several dives deep into sunless waters to feed on squid and small sharks.

All the world's oceans are connected—they are one big ocean. But that ocean contains many environments and an amazing variety of sea life.

Oceans

172

The ocean has different zones, or ranges of depth. The right whale strains its meal from the waters of the sunlit zone. Tiny organisms called algae drift there, using sunlight to make food. The algae, along with the tiny animals that feed on it, make up plankton (PLANGK tuhn), a "soup" of living things that drift with ocean currents. Right whales and other animals feed on the plankton.

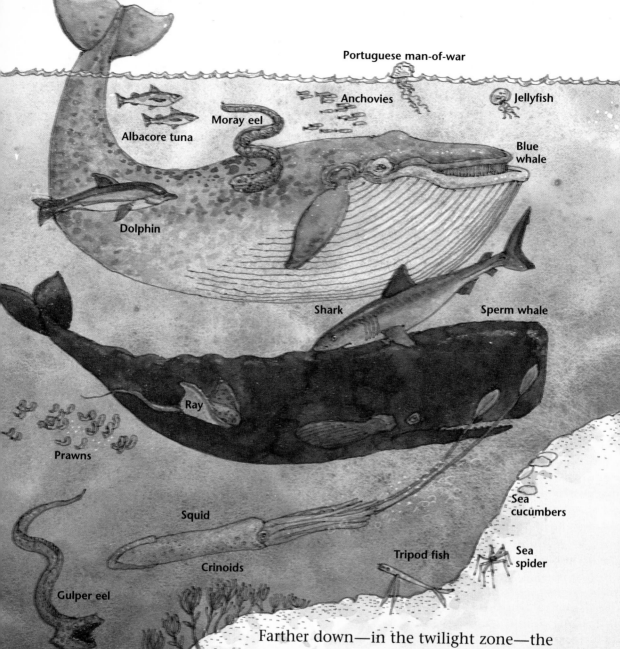

Portuguese man-of-war

Anchovies

Jellyfish

Moray eel

Albacore tuna

Blue whale

Dolphin

Shark

Sperm whale

Ray

Prawns

Squid

Sea cucumbers

Crinoids

Tripod fish

Sea spider

Gulper eel

Anglerfish

Venus's flower basket

Farther down—in the twilight zone—the sperm whale dives for its meals. Very little sunlight reaches these deep waters, so algae cannot grow there. Many creatures of the twilight zone are bioluminescent (BY uh LOO muh NEHS uhnt)—parts of their body light up—to attract prey. Some fish travel up to the surface at night to feed.

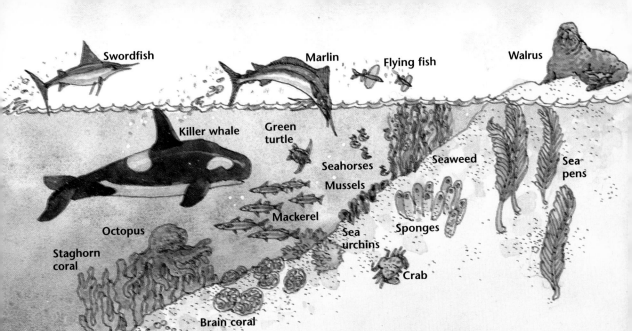

Swordfish

Marlin

Flying fish

Walrus

Killer whale

Green turtle

Seahorses

Seaweed

Sea pens

Mussels

Mackerel

Sponges

Octopus

Sea urchins

Staghorn coral

Crab

Brain coral

Starfish

Deeper still are the zones that no light reaches. The water is very cold, and the pressure would crush a human being. Food is so hard to find that some creatures have huge mouths and stomachs big enough to hold any meal that comes their way. Others wait for food to float down from above.

Some ocean habitats are close to land, and some are far out at sea. The coastal waters near continents are home to most of the ocean's animals. The water there is usually less than 500 feet (150 meters) deep, and sunlight sometimes reaches all the way to the sea floor. Rocks, seaweeds, and the sandy or muddy sea floor provide many homes and hiding places. Along tropical coasts, corals are found. Coral reefs provide food and shelter for many animals.

Far from land is the open ocean, where waters are deep. Flying fish, manta rays, sea turtles, sharks, dolphins, and many other animals live there.

How do animals live in the ocean?

In some ways, life in the ocean is easier than life on land. For one thing, warm areas of the ocean usually stay warm, and cold areas usually stay cold. So ocean animals don't have to adapt to changes in temperature. And they have all the water they need! But life in the ocean has other challenges.

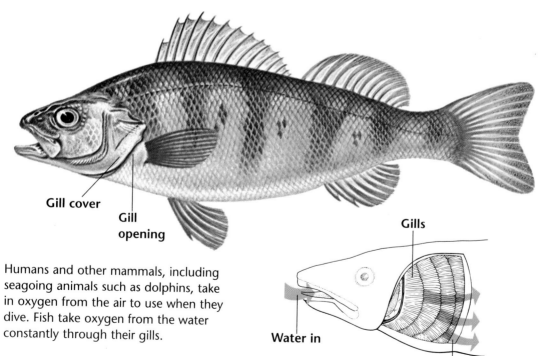

Gill cover

Gill opening

Gills

Water in

Water out

Humans and other mammals, including seagoing animals such as dolphins, take in oxygen from the air to use when they dive. Fish take oxygen from the water constantly through their gills.

How they get air

All animals need oxygen. Simple animals such as sea anemones (uh NEHM uh neez) absorb oxygen from water. Sea cucumbers pump water in and out of branching tubes called respiratory trees.

Many fish, shellfish, and other creatures have gills that take oxygen from water. Most fish breathe by pumping water over their gills. But tuna can't pump water. To move water over their gills, they swim fast with their mouths open. If they stopped, they would suffocate.

Seagoing mammals breathe air at the surface and then hold their breath underwater. Every breath has to last a long time. Weddell (WEHD uhl) seals can stay underwater for an hour! When they dive, their heartbeat slows, and blood goes to the brain and heart instead of to the muscles.

A starfish wraps its arms around a clam and then pulls it open to reach the tasty food inside.

Getting rid of salt

Some seashore animals have to filter their own water. Many places near the ocean have little or no fresh water, so these animals drink seawater. But

seawater is very salty, and salt in large doses is poisonous.

Some sea birds, such as petrels, gulls, terns, and albatrosses, have a special gland above their beak, near their eyes. This gland helps the bird get rid of salt through its nostrils. When the salty fluid drips out of their nostrils, many sea birds look as though they have a nasty cold.

Getting meals

Getting enough to eat can be a challenge anywhere, including the ocean. Some animals, like coral polyps, sponges, shellfish, and sea fans, filter food from the water. Parrot fish munch on coral and shellfish with their hard, beaklike mouths.

Sea urchins are a favorite meal for many sea creatures, but eating them is a challenge. Sea otters use rocks to bash them open. Blue triggerfish turn them upside down by blowing a jet of water at them. But the starfish just slides its stomach between the spines of the sea urchin and digests the soft middle. Then the starfish draws its stomach back in and moves on to the next victim.

Some of the largest ocean creatures eat some of the smallest ones. Gray, blue, and humpback

whales use their baleen—
the bony plates in their
mouths—to strain tiny plankton
from the water.

Other large creatures hunt bigger prey. Sperm whales, which have teeth, hunt for squid, their favorite food. Orcas, or killer whales, team up to hunt fish, seals, and even other whales. A pod of orcas sometimes herds salmon toward a rocky shore, and then swims into the school of trapped fish for easy feeding.

Unlike their relatives on land, sea turtles can swim swiftly through water to get a meal. They can do so because sea turtles have legs shaped like long paddles, or flippers. A dugong (DOO gahng), a sea mammal, uses its flippers to push tasty sea grass toward its mouth.

Pod (PAHD) is the name for a group of whales.

Some ocean creatures, such as cod, have sensitive whiskers. They use the whiskers to help them feel for small animals in the sediment on the sea floor.

Many deep-sea fish have glowing lures that attract unsuspecting prey into gulping range. Anglers have a fleshy bait that dangles above a wide mouth full of needle-sharp teeth. Any fish that goes for the bait is fast food for the angler.

Some fish have unusual weapons to catch food. Sawfish have a long snout edged with teeth. They slash through schools of fish and dine on the injured ones. They also use the snout to dig clams and other tasty morsels from the seafloor. Each kind of jellyfish has a certain number and length of tentacles. The tentacles contain stinging cells. When a small animal touches the tentacles, it becomes paralyzed and the jellyfish swallows its dinner.

A sea turtle (below) has flipperlike legs and feet. A land turtle (bottom) has clublike legs that are better for walking on sand, mud, or grass.

Sharks, the eating machines

Sharks are among the most feared predators in the ocean, and for good reason. Their bodies are perfectly designed for finding, catching, and gobbling prey.

Sharks' senses lead them straight to food. Take smell, for instance. Half of a shark's hourglass-shaped brain is used for smelling. A shark's sense of smell is so keen that it can smell one part of blood in a million parts of seawater.

A shark also has pores in its head that sense changes in pressure and temperature. And like most fish, it has a row of tiny canals on each side of its body, called lateral lines, that sense vibrations in the water. So sharks can find prey whether it's alive or dead, swimming or motionless.

Many of the larger sharks are constantly on the move. Unlike

All sharks are carnivores. Most of them eat live fish, but they can eat animals as small as plankton or as large as other sharks.

most fish, which pump water through their gills constantly, many sharks must keep moving to stay afloat and to keep water passing through their gills. And an excited shark can travel with great bursts of speed.

Once a shark finds its prey, its jaws open wide. They are hinged at the sides, top, and bottom, so a shark can swallow its prey whole. One account reports that an entire horse was found inside a huge great white shark.

Sharks have several rows of teeth. When a tooth falls out, another moves forward to replace it—a whole row of teeth may be replaced every week in some species. And a shark's digestive system is tough enough to dissolve metal.

People aren't sure where the word *shark* comes from. It may be related to the German word *Schurke,* which means "villain," or the old English word *sceran,* which means "to cut." Either way, the meaning is clear— don't mess with a shark.

You might think that since sharks are so fierce, they'd have no enemies. In fact, a shark's most common natural enemy is a bigger shark. But they have another enemy, too—human beings. Today, fishing crews catch so many that some kinds of sharks may become endangered.

Confusing the enemy

With so many animals looking for food, it's not always easy to avoid becoming a meal. So sea animals have developed some unusual ways of defending themselves.

Some creatures are equipped with poison. Stonefish are small, lumpy creatures that sit motionless on the sea floor, looking like stones and waiting to catch small fish. But their sting can be deadly. If threatened, they raise their back fins, which have stiff spines with poison-filled bulbs at the base. Anything, or anyone, unlucky enough to be stuck with one of these spines is in for an agonizing experience.

Other sea animals protect themselves by blending in with their surroundings. Their stripes, speckles, swirls, and whirls make them look like gravel, sand, or coral. Cuttlefish and their relatives—octopuses and squids—can change their colors and patterns to match almost any background.

And some sea animals have stopped looking like animals altogether. A type of seahorse called a leafy sea dragon has weedy fins, a bent body, and spiky ribs that make it look exactly like a kind of seaweed called kelp.

Leaf-shaped fins and a curving body make this sea dragon look like the fronds of seaweed that surround it.

Other animals have markings that confuse predators. Some fish have complicated patterns and some have false eyes—markings that look like eyes to a predator—or stripes that hide their real eyes. Butterfly fish have a large eyespot—an eye-shaped marking—near the base of the tail. Predators notice it and snap at the tail instead of the head. Butterfly fish even swim backward to confuse their enemies. When a predator aims for what looks like the front of the fish, the butterfly fish darts off in the other

HELPING HANDS

Coral reefs support so many animals that they are sometimes called the rain forests of the ocean. And like rain forests, many are endangered. Coral reefs around the island of Apo in the Philippines were almost completely destroyed by overfishing and by pollution. But a few years ago, island people established a coral sanctuary, a part of the reef where no fishing is allowed and anti-pollution regulations are strictly enforced. Now the fish and people are thriving and the reef is a popular scuba-diving attraction.

direction. The predator just gets a little bite of tail—if it's lucky.

Starfish and crabs can break off a limb or claw to escape from a predator. Some crabs use this defense against sea otters. When attacked, the crab clamps onto the otter and then breaks off its claw. While the otter is trying to pry off the claw, the crab makes its getaway. And then it grows a brand-new claw.

Marine neighborhood watch

Some animals use other animals to protect them. The blind shrimp depends on a small fish called a Luther's goby to guide it on food-gathering trips. The shrimp always keeps one feeler on the goby, which leads the shrimp toward food and away from danger. In exchange for this protection, the shrimp builds a burrow and shares it with the goby.

Pea crabs and hermit crabs use another animal for shelter. Some kinds of crab live inside the shell of a much larger clam, and other kinds move into the leftover shells of snails or sand dollars. Coral gall crabs make hollow chambers in coral. The female lives in the chamber and feeds on plankton that filters in.

The stinging tentacles of sea anemones provide protection for certain kinds of crabs. The crabs wear the anemones on their shells like flowers. Two claws of the boxer crab have evolved into permanent anemone-holders. The crab has to use its other claws to grab food. But if attacked, it waves its anemones at the attacker like living six-shooters.

Mangrove swamps

In some areas, land and ocean seem to mix. Close to the sea, the land gets wetter, and land plants give way to water-loving plants. The tides rise and fall, leaving the plants and animals in damp mud. Where rivers flow into the sea, fresh water and salty seawater mix, making brackish (BRAK ihsh) water. The plants and animals live in a habitat that is partly water and partly land, partly salty and partly fresh.

In tropical areas, mangrove swamps often grow. Mangrove trees thrive in salty water. Their tall, stilt-like roots anchor them in mud. The roots can live both underwater and out of water as the tide changes.

The mangroves provide a home for many creatures. Barnacles, oysters, and sea anemones fasten themselves to the roots. Crabs and small fish hide among them. Goggle-eyed fish called mudskippers

crawl onto the exposed roots, breathing oxygen from water stored in gill chambers.

Caterpillars and grubs bore into the mangrove's twigs. The tunnels they make provide shelter for spiders, insects, and scorpions. Birds and raccoons hunt among the branches. Leaves that fall into the water provide food and shelter for worms.

Larger animals live in mangrove swamps, too. Some aquatic mammals called manatees can live in either salt water or fresh water. These gentle giants can grow 13 feet (4 meters) long and weigh up to 3,500 pounds (1,600

kilograms). They eat huge amounts of water plants, which they grasp with their muscular lips or their front flippers.

Alligators and crocodiles are the main predators of the mangrove swamps of North and South America. Birds of prey such as ospreys and kites hunt small animals and fish. The fish in these swamps often include brackish-water species, such as barracudas, mangrove snappers, gobies, and sticklebacks. Mangrove swamps are also home to magnificent wading birds. Great blue herons stand 5 feet (1.5 meters) tall. Snowy egrets and scarlet ibises are a splendid sight. Roseate spoonbills stir the water with the spoon-shaped tips of their long beaks and snap up small animals.

Mangrove swamps thrive in a unique mix of salt water and fresh water, land and sea. They provide homes and food for fish and shellfish, insects, and a variety of birds and mammals.

Wild thing!

What is this wild creature? You will not find it anywhere in the ocean because it is not real. It is made up of special adaptations found in many different ocean creatures. Can you name the 10 adaptations and why they are important? Kudos to you if you can name one or two animals that have each adaptation!

Answers: 1. Crescent-shaped shark's tail is for speed; 2. Butterfly fish's false eye confuses enemies; 3. Crab's claw holds an anemone for protection; 4. Stonefish's sharp back fins are for protection; 5. Dugong's or turtle's flipper helps to move easily through the water and to gather food; 6. Fish's gills are for breathing underwater; 7. Octopus's body changes color for protection; 8. Angler's glowing lure attracts prey; 9. Seabird's special gland gets rid of salt; 10. Roseate spoonbill's wide beak stirs up water and snaps up snacks.

193

HUMANS
AND HABITATS

When people move animals

What happens when people introduce animals to new habitats?

Animals move from one habitat to another for many reasons. Some animals are fleeing predators or cold weather. Others are searching for food or a breeding place.

But sometimes people move animals for human reasons. Years ago, the British imported golden pheasants from China to provide food and sport. And fishing fans stocked far-flung lakes and rivers with rainbow trout from western North America.

Sometimes moving animals from their natural habitat saves them. For example, a certain kind of deer once lived only in the swamps of northern China. As rice farmers took over the wetlands, the

The Chinese call **Père David's deer** *ssu-pu-hsiang*, which means "the four unlikes." Why? It has the neck of a camel, the hoofs of a cow, the tail of a donkey, and the antlers of a deer.

wild deer disappeared. By 1865, all that remained was a captive herd in a park of the Chinese emperor. Père Armand David, a French missionary, had several deer from the herd shipped to England. Some were sent to zoos around the world. By 1921, the Chinese herd had died off. Only the Père David's deer in zoos survived.

However, the deer in zoos produced few young. To save the species, the Duke of Bedford gathered the deer in an English wildlife park at Woburn Abbey. There the herd grew and supplied animals to zoos. In 1957, the London Zoo sent four fawns to China to begin a new herd. Today, Père David's deer number more than 1,500 worldwide.

Bilbies (BIHL BEEZ) are one of Australia's more than 100 kinds of marsupials, or pouched mammals.

In some cases, animals become pests in their new habitats. During the 1850's, British settlers introduced rabbits to Australia. In Europe, rabbits feed on unwanted plants. This helps keep those plants from spreading. However, in Australia, much of the grassland is used for raising sheep. Rabbits there feed on, and destroy, the good pasture. They also take over the burrows of native animals such as bilbies, whose numbers are decreasing.

European starlings disturb habitats in North America. A group of people released starlings in New York City's Central Park in 1890, thinking that the birds would rid the surrounding countryside of crop-eating insects.

Unfortunately, starlings eat crops as well as insects. And, after a day of feeding, they flock to cities where they annoy residents by making lots of noise. Sometimes they even mimic ringing phones and shrieking sirens. They also harass woodpeckers, purple martins, and other birds by eating their food and taking over their nests.

When habitats are destroyed

What happens when people change animal habitats?

Ecotourism (EE kuh TOOR ihz uhm) is the business of nature travel. Some areas build their whole economy around a one-of-a-kind natural attraction.

Ecopreneurs (EE kuh pruh NURZ) are the people who work in ecotourism. They try to run the business so that tourists do not destroy the very sights that attract them.

Humans sometimes change animal habitats, and they usually do it for human reasons. Let's take a tour of some habitats that have changed. Of course, you'll see that storms and other natural disasters harm habitats. But people do more damage than nature does.

Our first stop is Prudhoe Bay on Alaska's Arctic coast. At one time, caribou came here to give birth. Now oil workers frighten away the caribou. The animals stay farther south, where they overgraze the land and suffer swarms of

insects. As a result, the herd produces fewer young than caribou in more remote parts of Alaska.

Another stop in Alaska is Prince William Sound. In 1989, a supertanker spilled almost 11 million gallons (42 million liters) of oil near its shore. The oil coated the seals' and sea otters' fur and the sea birds' feathers. Unable to swim or stay warm, thousands of animals drowned or froze. Whales and polar bears ate the sick and dying animals and swallowed poisons from the oil. These poisons are still in the food chain, sickening and killing animals.

A worker scoops up oil from a spill in Prince William Sound, Alaska. The oil is held inside a floating boom to keep it from spreading.

Northern spotted owl

Now let's go to a forest in California. Many of its evergreens are hundreds of years old. Northern spotted owls nest near the treetops and hunt on the forest floor. The owls need a wide range to find enough to eat, but only one-tenth of their habitat remains. Loggers cut down 60,000 acres (24,000 hectares) of old-growth trees every year. If the logging continues, the owls may disappear.

Logged-over forest

Take a look at this area in Texas. It was once grassland. Around 1900, it held a prairie dog town with a population of millions. Ranchers poisoned the prairie dogs because they grazed the same land as cattle. The ranchers didn't realize that prairie dogs destroy roots and shoots of shrubs and trees, leaving room for grass to grow. Today, the brush crowds out the grasses, and cattle have less grazing land.

West Texas grassland

Let's head east to Georgia's Okefenokee Swamp. A large company plans to build a strip mine at the swamp's edge. If they do, miners may pump up hundreds of thousands of gallons of ground water a day. This will lower the swamp's water level, leaving less food and shelter for egrets, alligators, and other animals that live in the swamp.

Alligator

Okefenokee Swamp

Prairie dog

Now let's cross the ocean to the national parks in Rwanda, Congo, and Uganda—the home of gorillas in the Virunga Mountains. At one time, local villagers wanted to use this area for cropland. However, in the 1980's, gorillas began to attract tourists, so villagers made their living from tourism instead. But since 1994, civil war has devastated the region and the tourist trade, and poachers as well as agriculture are now a major threat to gorillas.

Steer northeast to China. The last wild giant pandas live in the forest on China's Tibetan Plateau. These pandas eat mainly bamboo, which takes ten years or more to grow. In 1983, a large section of bamboo died out. A century ago, the pandas would have moved to another part of the forest. Today, miles of farms and villages separate the pandas from their food. Many pandas have starved to death.

The last stop is Australia. Can you spot the 3,307-mile (5,310-kilometer) fence from the Great Australian Bight to eastern Queensland? Sheep ranchers built this fence in 1960 to keep out dingoes, Australia's largest meat-eaters. Dingoes can't kill sheep inside the fence—but they can't kill kangaroos either. As a result, kangaroos have really multiplied. They compete with the sheep for grass and water and pose a bigger threat than the dingoes did.

Dingoes (DIHNG gohz) descend from a family of Asian dogs. The first people to arrive in Australia brought them as pets. They have run wild in the Australian outback for thousands of years.

A long dingo-proof fence, Australia

Dingo

When humans care for animal habitats

What are people doing to help animals' habitats?

People called conservationists (KAHN suhr VAY shuhn ihsts) regard animals as beautiful, valuable, interesting, and necessary. Conservationists work to save animals and their habitats.

During the 1950's and 1960's, runoff from British farms carried a pesticide into rivers. Runoff is water from rain or snow that runs off the land. The bug killer in this runoff poisoned the fish and the European otters who ate them. By 1978, otters were disappearing from Britain. Conservationists urged farmers to stop using the pesticide and pressured local officials to clean up the rivers. Now a group called the Otter Trust is breeding otters and restoring them to clean waters.

Sometimes, there are not enough homes in an animal's habitat. For example, macaws in Peru typically nest in old, tall trees. The birds prefer high, dry holes to discourage predators and protect their chicks. But many old trees in the rain forest were cut down. Afterward, many macaws were homeless. To save them, conservationists developed nesting boxes where the birds nest and raise their young.

A conservationist hoists a nesting box high into a rain forest tree (left) and introduces a macaw to its new home (below).

Conservationists also pressure government leaders to set aside preserves and parks where little or no hunting and development are allowed. Today, jaguars stake out territories in Brazil's Jau National Park. Giant pandas wander forests in Wolong, China's largest panda reserve. Asian tigers stalk in Nepal's Royal Chitwan National Park. Large herds of African antelope, elephants, and other grass-eaters roam Serengeti National Park in Tanzania.

To keep animals protected and happy in a zoo, workers try to re-create natural habitats, including climates. In a penguin habitat, for example, refrigeration systems chill the artificial rock landscape. As water streams across the rock, it freezes and forms real ice.

Rain forest habitats in zoos may have trees made of fiberglass. Real plants and vines hang from the "trees" and make ideal swings for monkeys.

Some zoos clean their animals' swimming areas with ozone rather than fish-killing chlorine. Fish can live in ozone-treated water, so polar bears can hunt them as they would in the wild.

Zoo workers try to re-create an animal's natural habitat, using artificial landscapes and special heating and cooling devices. Later, they'll add real and artificial plants.

Sometimes zoo-bred animals are returned to their natural habitats. For example, zoos around the world cooperate to bring animals such as the deerlike Arabian oryx back to the grasslands of Oman, and Przewalski's horse back to Mongolia. Both kinds of animals had disappeared from the wild before zoos stepped in.

Zoos also educate people about animals. They allow people to observe wild animals close up. This closeness encourages people to care about animals and their problems. What better way to gain new conservationists?

Wild animals in zoos need some special care. This zookeeper is filing an elephant's toenails. In the wild, the nails would have worn down naturally.

How the porcupine got its quills

Some animals are not very strong or swift. Yet they can survive in a habitat shared with strong predators, swift prey, and even people. This Seneca Indian tale tells how one animal managed to find and keep a special place in its habitat.

There once was an animal called Gray One. He had a soft gray coat, he was cheerful and kind, and he was never in a hurry.

But other animals were impatient with him because he moved so slowly. "Hurry up," Bear would say. "Get out of my way."

"But I don't like to hurry," Gray One would reply.

So Bear would walk right over him, stepping on him with his heavy clawed feet.

"Don't block the path," Bobcat would snarl at him.

"But it's my path—I made it," Gray One would explain.

Then Bobcat would grab him with his sharp-clawed paws and fling him aside.

And so it went.

One day Red Fox saw Gray One licking his scratches and bruises. "Gray One, who fought with you?" he said.

"No one," Gray One said, and sighed. "They all scratch and bite me."

"Never mind that," said Fox. "Will you do me a favor? Pick me a pine cone from that tree."

Gray One climbed up easily and picked him a perfect pine cone.

"Thank you," said Fox. "You're a fine fellow. Would you like to be my friend?"

"And your breakfast?" said Gray One.

"No, I won't eat you," said Fox. "I don't make friends very often, but I do like you. And I can help you."

"How?" said Gray One.

"First, roll in that mud," said Fox.

"And get my fur all sticky?" Gray One asked.

"As sticky as you can," said Fox.

"Is this a trick?" said Gray One. "Are you going to claw me?"

"Don't worry," said Fox.

So Gray One did it. Fox laughed. "You look like a big blob of clay," he said. "That's exactly what I need. Now hold still."

Fox pulled some thorns off a hawthorn tree. He pushed them into Gray One's muddy coat, with the points sticking out all over.

"Now," said Fox, "I'm going to sit on this rock. You do just as I say."

"Do what?" said Gray One.

"Just what you always do. Stay in your path."

Soon Bear came along. Hunting had been bad, and he was grouchy. "Out of my way, Gray One," he said.

"I don't like to hurry," said Gray One.

"Then I'll hurry you!" said Bear.

"Go ahead, Bear," called Fox. "Toss him out of the way."

Bear grabbed Gray One. "Gr-ouch! Ouch!" he roared. "You've stuck my hands through and through." And off he hopped, shaking his wounded paws.

Then along came Bobcat, who was always cross. "Out of my way, Gray One," he yowled.

"I'll stay right here," said Gray One, who was beginning to like his new coat.

"No, you won't," screeched Bobcat, and gave Gray One a bite. "Scr-ouch! What-t-t's this-s-s in my mou-ou-outh?" Away he ran, clawing at his mouth to pull out the thorns.

And so it went with every animal that came along Gray One's path.

"So now," Fox said, "I have made you strong. The pine cone you gave me is magic and gives me speed. The new coat I gave you will let you take your time and make your own path."

And now Porcupine takes his time, and anyone who quarrels with him gets a skinful of troubles.

Glossary

Here are some words you have read in this book. You can see how to say them in the parentheses after the word: **insulation** (IHN suh LAY shuhn). Say the parts in small letters more softly, those in small capital letters a little louder, and those in large capital letters loudest. Following the pronunciation are one or two sentences that tell the meaning of the word as it is used in this book.

adapt (uh DAPT) To fit in with a new condition or place; to become suited to something.

alpine zone (AL pyn ZOHN) The zone at the highest altitude, above the timber line, where only small plants grow.

amphibian (am FIHB ee uhn) A cold-blooded animal with a backbone and usually a smooth, moist skin. Many amphibians are born in water but later live on land.

antennae (an TEHN ee) Long, slender feelers on the head of an insect, centipede, scorpion, or lobster. The singular is antenna (an TEHN uh).

bacteria (bak TIHR ee uh) Kinds of simple living things so small that they can usually be seen only with a microscope.

browser (BROWZ uhr) An animal that eats entirely or mostly leaves, shoots, and bark of trees and shrubs.

camouflage (KAM uh flahzh) Protective colorings or markings that help conceal an animal in its surroundings.

canopy (KAN uh pee) The rooflike topmost layer of growth formed by the tallest trees in a forest, which shades the lower layers.

carnivore (KAHR nuh vawr) An animal that eats only or mostly meat.

coniferous (kuh NIHF uhr uhs) Having their seeds in cones. Pine trees are coniferous.

consumer (kuhn SOO muhr) Any living thing that eats food. All animals are consumers.

deciduous (dih SIHJ oo uhs) Shedding all leaves and growing new leaves each year.

forage (FOHR ihj) To search about for food.

gill (gihl) A part of the body with thin walls that fish, crabs, tadpoles, and other water animals use to breathe. The gills take in oxygen from the water.

grub (gruhb) The wormlike larva of an insect.

habitat (HAB uh tat) The place where a particular kind of living thing naturally lives and grows.

herbivore (HUHR buh vawr) An animal that eats only or mostly plants.

hibernate (HY buhr nayt) To spend a cold season in a deep sleep. When animals hibernate, their body temperature lowers and their breathing and heartbeat slow down.

insulation (IHN suh LAY shuhn) A material that does not conduct heat in or out. In animals, fur or fat serves as insulation against losing heat in cold weather.

invertebrate (ihn VUHR tuh briht) Without a backbone. Animals such as worms, insects, and jellyfish are invertebrates.

lichen (LY kuhn) A plantlike living thing that is a kind of algae and a fungus growing together. Lichen grows on rocks, trees, and other surfaces.

migrate (MY grayt) To move from one place to another as seasons change.

mollusk (MAHL uhsk) One of a large group of animals with no backbone, a soft body, and usually a hard outer shell. Snails and clams are mollusks.

nectar (NEHK tuhr) A sweet liquid found in many flowers. Some insects and birds feed on nectar.

omnivore (AHM nuh vawr) An animal that eats both animals and plants as part of its regular diet.

prehensile (pree HEHNS uhl) Able to hold or grasp.

producer (pruh DOO suhr) Any living thing that produces food. All green plants are producers.

rodent (ROH duhnt) Any of a large group of mammals with two large, strong front teeth for gnawing. Mice, rats, beavers, and squirrels are rodents.

savanna (suh VAN uh) A grassy plain with scattered trees, often lying between tropical forestland and desert.

scavenger (SKAV uhn juhr) An animal that feeds on dead animals. Vultures, jackals, and some insects are scavengers.

snow line (SNOH lyn) The height on mountains above which there is always snow.

temperate (TEHM puhr iht) Neither very hot nor very cold.

timber line (TIHM buhr LYN) The height on mountains or the distance north or south in polar regions beyond which trees will not grow.

vertebrate (VUHR tuh briht) Having a backbone. Mammals, birds, reptiles, fish, and amphibians are vertebrates.

Find Out More

There are so many exciting resources about animals, you are sure to find plenty to enjoy. The ones listed here are only a sampling. Your school or public library will have many more.

Ages 5-8

Animal Omnibus
http://www.birminghamzoo.com/ao/
This Web site, sponsored by the Birmingham Zoo, is a list of Web sources indexed by the animal's common name. It's easy for even the young child to find links for more information on all kinds of animals.

The Animals
on CD-ROM for Mac/Windows (Mindscape, 1995)
See and hear more than 200 exotic mammals, birds, and reptiles through video clips as you learn more from the experts at the San Diego Zoo.

Crinkleroot's Guide to Knowing Animal Habitats
by Jim Arnosky (Simon & Schuster, 1997)
Take a trip with Crinkleroot and you will learn more about habitats—from lowlands to mountains, wetlands to drylands.

Learning About Animals
CD-ROM for Mac/Windows (Orange Cherry New Media, 1997)
In this CD-ROM you'll learn more about how animals can adapt to various habitats and climates. You'll also learn about animal classification.

Picture Reference: Animals
by Janine Amos (World Book,1997)
Packed with large, detailed illustrations, this colorful reference book provides an exciting introduction to the animal kingdom.

Powerful Beasts of the Wild
by Theresa Greenaway (DK, 1997)
You'll learn more about wild animals and their habitats from the American bison to the red kangaroos of Australia. Beautiful photos illustrate this easy-to-read text.

Temperate Forest Mammals
by Elaine Landau (Children's Press, 1996)
Temperate forests have warm summers and cold winters. This author introduces you to five animals that make their home in this environment: beavers, echidnas, raccoons, koalas, and wild boars. Other titles in this True Books series include *Tropical Forest Mammals* and *Mountain Mammals*.

Underwater Animals
by Helen Cooney (Time-Life, 1996)
Crabs, lobsters, sharks, and eels are only some of the animals that make their home underwater. In this book, you'll read about these animals and many more.

Ages 9 and Up

ABC World Experience: Wide World of Animals,
CD-ROM for Mac/Windows
(Creative Wonders, 1996)
More than 700 species of animals are included in this CD that uses text, photos, sound clips, and full-screen videos. You will learn interesting facts about animal characteristics, observe them in their natural habitat, and discover threats to their survival.

Animals of the Desert
by Stephen Savage (Raintree Steck-Vaughn, 1997)
This book tells you about mammals, birds, reptiles, amphibians, and invertebrates who have adapted to harsh desert conditions. This title is part of the Animals by Habitat series.

Chameleons on Location
by Kathy Darling (Lothrop, Lee and Shepard, 1997)
Fifty-three of the 128 known species of chameleons are found in the endangered rain forests of Madagascar. The author and her photographer daughter traveled to this area where they studied this fascinating lizard.

Endangered Tigers
by Amanda Harman (Benchmark, 1996)
Tigers are in danger of becoming extinct because people hunt them and destroy their forest homes. The author describes the different habitats where tigers live and tells about what is being done to save these animals.

Rainforest Explorer
CD-ROM for Mac/Windows
(Orange Cherry New Media, 1995)
Video and photography bring to life the animals and plants of the rain forest. This CD also explains the dangers that face this natural resource.

Sea World Busch Gardens Animal Resources
http://www.bev.net/education/seaworld/infobook.html
"Endangered Species," "Polar Bears," "Tropical Forests," and "Careers" are only a few of the links that this Web site makes available. With a click of the mouse, you can take an aquatic safari!

What's a Penguin Doing in a Place Like This?
by Miriam Schlein (Millbrook Press, 1997)
Believe it or not, not all penguins live in ice and snow! There are seventeen different kinds of penguins. Although they all make their homes south of the equator, some live on a tropical island where the temperature is usually over 100° F.

World Book Looks At Insects and Spiders
(World Book, 1996)
In this book, children will find colorful pictures, easy-to-read text, and facts that will fascinate, amuse, and inform. A journey of discovery through the world of knowledge, this book is part of the World Book Looks At series.

Index

This index is an alphabetical list of important topics covered in this book. It will help you find information given in both words and pictures. To help you understand what an entry means, there is sometimes a helping word in parentheses, for example, **addaxes** (antelopes). If there is information in both words and pictures, you will see the words *with pictures* in parentheses after the page number. If there is only a picture, you will see the word *picture* in parentheses after the page number.

Illustration Acknowledgments

The publishers of *Childcraft* gratefully acknowledge the courtesy of the following photographers, agencies, and organizations for the illustrations in this volume. When all the illustrations for a sequence of pages are from a single source, the inclusive page numbers are given. Credits should be read from left to right, top to bottom, on their respective pages. All illustrations are the exclusive property of the publishers of *Childcraft* unless names are marked with an asterisk (*).

Cover   Aristocrat, Discovery, and Standard Bindings—Paul Turnbaugh
Heritage Binding—Frans Lanting, Minden Pictures*; Paul Turnbaugh; George Ulrich; Paul Turnbaugh; Malcolm Ellis; Paul Turnbaugh; George Ulrich; © Gerry Ellis, ENP Images*; Paul Turnbaugh

10–11   © Glenn Randall*
12–15   John Sandford
16–17   Richard Kaneiss
18–21   George Ulrich
22–23   © Glenn Randall*; © Michael Durham, ENP Images*; © William Grentell, Visuals Unlimited*
24–25   Drew-Brook-Cormack
26–27   WORLD BOOK art; Tom Dolan; Richard Lewington, The Garden Studio; Stanley W. Galli; James Teason; Trevor Boyer, Linden Artists Ltd.; John D. Dawson; WORLD BOOK art
28–29   Yoshi Miyake
30–31   John Sandford; © Stephen Dalton, Photo Researchers*; © Mike Andrews, Animals Animals*
32–33   © Konrad Wothe, ENP Images*
34–35   John Sandford
36–41   John Sandford
42–43   © F. Gohier, Photo Researchers*; © David Woodfall, ENP Images*
44–45   John Sandford
46–47   Margaret L. Estey; Pedro Julio Gonzales; © Robert Maier, Animals Animals*
48–49   Drew-Brook-Cormack
50–51   Pedro Julio Gonzales; © Darek Karp, NHPA*; © Joe Mac Donald, Visuals Unlimited*
52–53   Drew-Brook-Cormack; Robert Morton
54–55   John Sandford; © Howard Buffett, BioImages*; Stanley W. Galli
56–57   © Frans Lanting, Minden Pictures*
58–59   John Sandford
60–61   John Sandford
62–63   © Howard Buffett, BioImages*; © Hamman Heldring, Animals Animals*
64–65   © Mitsuaki Iwago, Minden Pictures*; © Gerry Ellis, ENP Images*; © Michael Edwards*
66–67   John Sandford
68–69   © Clem Haagner/ABPL from Photo Researchers*; Robert Morton
70–71   Robert Morton
72–73   © Mitsuaki Iwago, Minden Pictures*; © Rod Planck, Photo Researchers*; © Howard Buffett, BioImages*
74–77   John Sandford
78–79   © Michael Durham, ENP Images*
80–83   John Sandford
84–85   Richard Orr; © Stephen Dalton, Animals Animals*
86–87   © Kevin Shafer*; © Nigel Smith, Animals Animals*; © Konrad Wothe, ENP Images*
88–89   © Patti Murray, Animals Animals*; Paul Lopez
90–91   Robert Morton
92–93   © Kevin Shafer*; Richard Hook
94–95   John Sandford; © P. Delance-Saola, Gamma/Liaison*
96–97   John Sandford; Wendy Smith-Griswold
98–101   John Sandford
102–103   © Michio Hashino, Minden Pictures*
104–105   WORLD BOOK map; John Sandford
106–107   John Sandford
108–109   Robert Morton

110–111   Peter Barrett; © Carson Baldwin, Jr., Animals Animals*; © Ted Levin, Animals Animals*
112–113   © S. Michael Biscelglie, Animals Animals*; © Ron Sanford, Tony Stone Images*; Jean Cassels
114–115   John Sandford
116–117   © Bryan & Cherry Alexander*
118–119   Richard Orr; © Randall Hyman*
120–121   Drew-Brook-Cormack
122–123   John Sandford; © Mitsuaki Iwago, Minden Pictures*
124–125   © Tui De Roy, Minden Pictures*
126–129   John Sandford
130–131   Malcolm Ellis; © David Selk, ENP Images*; © Frans Lanting, Minden Pictures*; © Bruce Davidson, Animals Animals*
132–133   © Daniel Hevclin, NHPA*; © R. F. Ashley, Visuals Unlimited*; Richard Orr
134–135   © Mitsuaki Iwago, Minden Pictures*; Drew-Brook-Cormack; © Dennis Paulson, Visuals Unlimited*
136–137   John Sandford; Tony Gibbons
138–139   © Michael Fogden, Animals Animals*; Richard Orr
140–141   © Mickey Gibson, Animals Animals*
142–143   John Sandford; © Jones & Shimlock, NHPA*
144–147   George Ulrich
148–149   © Walt Enders, ENP Images*
150–151   John Sandford
152–153   John Sandford
154–155   George Ulrich
156–157   © Joe McDonald, Bruce Coleman, Ltd*; © Tom Ulrich, Tony Stone Images*
158–159   © Jean-Louis LeMoigne, NHPA*; Drew-Brook-Cormack
160–161   WORLD BOOK art; John Charles Pitcher
162–163   Drew-Brook-Cormack; © Art Wolfe, Tony Stone Images*
164–165   © Glenn M. Oliver, Visuals Unlimited*; © Michael K. Nicholas, National Geographic Society*;
166–167   Drew-Brook-Cormack
168–169   John Sandford; © Renee Lynn, Tony Stone Images*
170–171   © Jeremy Stafford-Deitsch, ENP Images*
172–173   John Sandford
174–175   John Sandford
176–177   James Teason; Margaret Ann Moran; George Ulrich
178–179   © Fred Bavendam*
180–181   Tony Gibbons; © William M. Stephens, Tom Stack & Associates*; © Steve Winter, National Geographic Society*
182–183   John Sandford; © Dave B. Fleetham, Visuals Unlimited*
184–185   © Fred Bavendam*
186–187   Tony Gibbons; © Carl Roessler*
188–189   John Sandford
190–191   John Sandford: Wendy Smith-Griswold
192–193   John Sandford
194–195   © Gerry Ellis, ENP Images*
196–199   John Sandford
200–201   © Alan Levenson, Tony Stone Images*
202–203   © William Campbell, Sygma*; Robert Morton; © Douglas Kirkland, Sygma*; Robert Morton; © John D. Cunningham, Visuals Unlimited*
204–205   © Medford Taylor, National Geographic Society*; Robert Morton
206–207   © Frans Lanting, Minden Pictures*
208–209   Brookfield Zoo*; © Bert Buxbaum, Columbus Zoo*
210–215   John Sandford

World Book Encyclopedia, Inc., provides high-quality educational and reference products for the family and school, including a six-volume **Childcraft favorite set** with colorful books on favorite topics such as **dogs** and **prehistoric animals**; and **The World Book/Rush-Presbyterian-St. Luke's Medical Center Medical Encyclopedia**, a 1,072-page, fully illustrated family health reference. For further information, write World Book Encyclopedia, Attention Customer Service, Post Office Box 11207, Des Moines, IA 50340-1207. Or, visit our Web site at http://www.worldbook.com